CALLED OUT

Dismantling The Occult & Living
with The Power of Jesus As Your
Normal

JAMAL MAXSAM

Unless otherwise indicated, Bible quotations are taken from The New American Standard Bible®, Copyright © 1960, 1971, 1977, 1995, 2020 by The Lockman Foundation. Used by permission. All rights reserved. lockman.org"

Scriptures indicated AMPC, NKJV, KJV, TPT are from:
The Amplified® Bible (AMPC), Copyright © 19541958, 1962, 1964, 1965, 1987 by The Lockman Foundation Used by permission. lockman.org
The New King James Version®. Copyright © 1982 by Thomas Nelson. Used by permission. All rights reserved.
The Passion Translation®. Copyright © 2017, 2018, 2020 by Passion & Fire Ministries, Inc. Used by permission. All rights reserved. ThePassionTranslation.com.
The King James Version of the Bible. Public domain.
ISBN: Paperback: 979-8-9991499-0-9

E-book: 979-8-9991499-0-9

Published By: Jamal Maxsam, LLC
Cincinnati, OH
Editor and Interior Design: Deborah A Gaston,
Photographer: Bonnie Kratzer

For the ones who walk in intimacy with Jesus, living in His power as their new normal, and for the ones set free from the shadows of the occult—past, present, and future—this book is dedicated to you. I honor your journey, and I celebrate your freedom in Christ.

ENDORSEMENTS

I highly encourage you to read and study *Called Out*. If you do, be prepared to be challenged. If you live more in religion than in relationship, not only will this book be challenging, but it will also show you the path to move from religion to living out a relational Kingdom of God lifestyle, characterized by truth, mercy, forgiveness, signs, miracles, and wonders on a daily basis. Should you read it, after you finish it, I suggest that you pray daily that God will use you to be the answer to someone else's prayer and hold on (in such a good way) as you discern His Kingdom in relationship with Him daily.

Jamal, thank you for the courage, humility, and vulnerability that you live in your life, and especially for putting yourself at risk by putting these truths on paper. Well done, my friend!
Ford Taylor, FSH Consulting LLC,
Author and Founder: Transformational Leadership Training and Consulting (TL), "Relacional Leadership" and the Missing Link (ML)

For nearly twenty years, I have had the privilege of knowing Pastor Jamal Maxsam—not just as a friend, but as a co-laborer in ministry. He is a faithful servant of God, a powerful teacher, and a courageous leader who walks in unwavering commitment to truth. In *Called Out*, Jamal has written what the Body of Christ desperately needs in this hour—a clear path to freedom that exposes deception and points people directly to the liberating power of Jesus Christ.

We're living in confusing times spiritually. Everywhere you look, there are new belief systems, old occult practices dressed up in modern language, and deceptive teachings that sound good but lead people away from God. What makes Jamal's voice so powerful is that he's not guessing about this darkness—he lived in it, was dramatically rescued by Jesus, and now speaks with the authority of someone who has been genuinely set free.

This book will bring healing to the wounded, freedom to the captive, and deliverance to those trapped by spiritual deception. More importantly, it will show believers that living with Jesus as LORD isn't just for Sunday morning—it's meant to be our normal, everyday experience.
Read this book. Apply what God reveals to you through these pages. And refuse to settle for anything less than the full freedom Jesus purchased for you on the cross. The enemy has deceived too many for too long. It's time for God's people to walk in the power and victory that already belongs to them. This book will show you how.
Nick Stevenson
Associate Pastor, Charis Church

Here's a shout-out for *Called Out!* This is a powerful book that deserves to be on every Christian's reading list. Jamal Maxsam's personal story provides riveting context. Still, everyone fortunate enough to read this will learn a great deal about how to hear God's authentic voice, and how to walk in Kingdom authority.
Chuck Proudfit
President, At Work On Purpose

In a world filled with spiritual distractions and deception, this book offers a clear and powerful roadmap to true freedom. Jamal Maxsam masterfully uncovers the insidious nature of occult influences and points readers directly to the liberating power of Jesus Christ. This is not just a book to be read, but a spiritual guide to truth. Prepare for deliverance, revelation, and an unshakeable foundation in the truth.
Nina Marie Neal, Prophet and Pastor, HEIRS Covenant Church
The teacher is in the house! Prepare to experience truth as Jamal

challenges your understanding of the transactions of the spirit as he dismantles beliefs of the occult brick by brick.
Pastor Derick Thomas, Presence Driven Churchhouse

Contents

ACKNOWLEDGMENTS

First, I thank my wife, Valerie. I love you. Thank you for walking with me on this exciting journey of faith and the miraculous in the Lord. Together, we will continue to experience the goodness and faithfulness of God as He brings His Word to pass in and through our lives.

To my daughter Shay—you are a blessing from God. I love you. To my son-in-law, Tysson, continue to grow as the man of God you were designed to be. And to my grandson, Baby O., I love you and can't wait to see all that God will do in and through you. The ground I take becomes your starting point.

To my apostle, pastor, mentor, and spiritual father, Apostle John W. Stevenson—thank you for your encouragement and for modeling what it means to live from a Kingdom perspective. You challenge me, help me grow, and hold me accountable. I am deeply grateful for your influence and example. You and Mom are a tremendous blessing in my life.

To Pastor Deborah A. Gaston, thank you for mentoring me in the prophetic, for loving me, encouraging me in my walk with God, and for your editorial work on this project. You lovingly challenge me not to say too much on paper (haha). I love and appreciate you.

To my HEIRS Covenant Church family—I love you all. HEIRS is a special place because of you. Together, we get to steward God's Presence and experience Him in incredible ways each time we gather. Thank you for being who you are. Collectively, we have the privilege of advancing the Kingdom of God in every sphere of life.

To my Champion University family—I love each one of you. I'm grateful that we get to walk and grow together. It's an honor to do life with you as we operate in the power of Jesus as our normal.

Thank you for trusting me to mentor you. Signs follow you as you believe.

To Pastors Michael and Shirley Joyce, thank you for loving me and for teaching me the principles of faith.

To my Kingdom Builders Family—Kellee Williams, Paul Ybarra, and April Nicole Scipio—I love you and your families deeply. You are incredible gifts to the Body of Christ and to my life. You are truly my Kingdom siblings. Your love, support, prayers, and encouragement mean more than words can express. I'm so grateful that God connected us and allows us to do life together.

Kellee, thank you for your sensitivity to Holy Spirit and for your obedience in encouraging me to teach on the supernatural at a time when I was wrestling with the assignment.

To my biological family, I love you all. To those walking with Jesus, keep living by faith and growing in your relationship with Him. To those who have not yet received Him as Lord and Savior, my prayer is that you will. May my journey draw you closer to a place of surrender to Him. He loves you—and has loved you from before you were born.

To my grandmother and mother, now with Jesus in Heaven—I love and honor you. You were called to be prophets who revealed Jesus to those in your sphere of influence. Though you did not fulfill the full measure of that call, I honor who you were. As I walk out my assignment, I recognize that I am also stepping into what was meant for you—fulfilling your unfinished assignments alongside my own and redeeming what was lost. The blood of Jesus has redeemed your legacy.

Finally, to Jesus Christ, my Lord, Savior, and God—thank You for loving me, for being with me, for revealing Yourself to me, calling me, and choosing me. I get to do life with You as You demonstrate Your Kingdom and draw others to Yourself. Thank You for being my best friend and allowing me to encounter Your Presence in such tangible ways.

All glory to You, Lord.

PREFACE

This book has been in the making for a long time. I have been prayerfully waiting for the moment when Holy Spirit would release me to share it with you. Over ten years ago, God spoke to me: *"I want you to write a book about your testimony."* When I heard those words, my heart raced. I was nervous, wondering if anyone would believe me—or think differently about me—because of my past experiences.

While I share only a portion of my journey, I've included enough for anyone operating in spiritualism, the occult, or any practice contrary to Scripture to receive their freedom. It is my desire that every believer who reads this book will grow in discernment and develop a deeper hunger to walk in the power of Jesus as their normal—never settling for a powerless relationship.

I wrote *Called Out* to share principles of operating in the miraculous power of Jesus as a normal way of life. I've found that many believers are unaware that this dimension is available to them. We do not have to wait for a special service, a conference, or a well-known person to see miracles happen.

Some have such an intense desire to see miracles that they miss the reality that God desires to use them to work miracles. I believe it is time for believers to shift from asking for miracles to walking in Kingdom authority to perform them.

We were not designed to be weak or powerless. We are designed to walk in power as we demonstrate the reality of God's Kingdom and the resurrection power of Jesus. God created the spiritual realm, and through Jesus, we have authority in it. We should not seek spiritual experiences or follow teachings that do not align with His Word. As we seek God according to Scripture, we will encounter Him in supernatural ways. One of the great deceptions of our time is that many unknowingly engage in spiritual practices, believing they are following God, when in reality they are being led by deceptive spirits. These spirits aim to create counterfeit encounters that pull people away from God instead of drawing them closer to Him.

I experienced firsthand what it's like to engage in spiritual practices, believing they were of God, only to realize they were not. I also know what it feels like to crave more of God, to sense there is more to Jesus than emotional hype or religious routine.

In this book, I share candidly about my background in spiritualism and how, by His mercy, grace, and unfailing love, God intervened and freed me from that demonic deception. I also share some of the lessons He has taught me about operating in the supernatural as part of our covenant relationship with Jesus.

To protect the identities of those involved in some of my experiences, I've changed names throughout the book. While *Called Out* dismantles spiritualist teachings, it is not the purpose of this book to expose individuals. Some have not yet come to know Jesus as Lord and Savior, and I have chosen to use wisdom to ensure that fulfilling this assignment does not interfere with what God may be doing in their lives as He draws them to Himself.

However, I do share the name of the founder of the organization I was once a part of. I do this to warn you about the dangerous teachings it promotes and to reveal how one person's deception can negatively affect countless lives for generations.

It is my prayer that *Called Out* is a blessing and a tool in your personal walk with Jesus. May the truths within draw you into deeper intimacy with Him. May God use you in the miraculous to point people to Him and bring souls into His Kingdom.

CHAPTER 1

THE QUESTION THAT BROKE MY CHAINS

"If what you believe is true... then why this?"
God asked me this question three times during an encounter I will never forget. It was the first time I audibly heard His voice. That encounter, much like the Apostle Paul's encounter on the road to Damascus, changed my life forever. At the age of 17, I surrendered to Jesus as my Savior and Lord, and I have walked with Him ever since.

Drawn by Grace from Deception to Truth

I grew up in spiritualism; it was the framework that shaped me as a child. I was convinced that we worshiped Jesus. It's easy to believe the lie and live in deception when that's all you've ever known. It becomes the reality from which you live and view the world, and that was my reality. I didn't realize I was in bondage to a lie.

God's desire, however, is that we know the truth, for it is truth that makes us free (John 8:31-32). He does not want anyone to perish; He wants all to have eternal life, life abundant that is only found in Jesus Christ. And He will invade any space, any place, and use anyone He chooses, to reveal Truth—Jesus— to us and draw us to Him. Through His love, grace, mercy, and wisdom, He draws the spiritualist, like I once was, and others mired in deception to Himself.

He did that for me in the most undeniable way.

An Unlikely Place to Be Saved

I was attending a convention in Detroit, Michigan, the headquarters of the organization to which my family was affiliated. It was one of the two annual conventions that brought all the "churches" together. I always looked forward to them. I truly believed I was learning about God, and I always expected the conferences to be powerful.

The main building on the grounds resembled an old Catholic church, with three large sections of seating, a pulpit, and an altar with candles and incense. Looming over the altar was a 10-foot portrait of the founder, George Hurley. As a child, it seemed the eyes of that portrait followed me; I sensed a spiritual presence that frightened and unsettled me.

My family and I had been at the convention all day. Services ran from morning to night, and I was tired and restless, as any 17-year-old would be. So, I slipped outside just for an escape, trying to avoid anyone who might tell my grandmother or mother, who both held high positions in the organization, that I had left the meeting.

If What You Believe is True… Then?

Suddenly, as I was walking, a bright light surrounded me; the brilliance seemed to swallow me and the world around me. I heard a Voice—not imagined, not internal, but audible and undeniable.

"If what you believe is true… then why this?"

I knew it was the voice of Jesus.

Immediately, I had a vision. I was back in a service I'd attended as a child. A woman—known as a witch—entered the sanctuary, interrupting everything. She marched to the pulpit, seized the microphone, and said: "God is a jealous God, and He is tired of you calling on the name of someone else."

"Get out of here!" someone shouted. Others grumbled

"You better listen. It will cost you your life," the witch declared. The room fell quiet; the silence was palpable.

The leaders all sat as still and quiet as everyone else. I thought, "With all the master-level mediums sitting here, why aren't they doing anything?"

"God is a jealous God," the witch repeated. "And He is tired of you calling on the name of someone else."

She returned the mic to the stand and walked out, the doors thundering shut behind her.

No one moved. No one spoke. And once the woman was gone, they carried on as if nothing had happened.

I was baffled. Why hadn't the leaders, with all the power they claimed to possess, done something?

Then I heard the voice again: *"If what you believe is true... then why this?"*

Another vision came. Three men were breaking into the fellowship hall, stealing the "sacred" items— candle holders, incense burners, valuable items of gold, silver, copper, and bronze.

I'd asked myself, "How could they break into what was supposed to be the House of God, steal sacred items, and get away with it, especially after all the displays of spiritual power I've witnessed and even performed myself?"

A third time the LORD asked, *"If what you believe is true... then why this?"*

By then, I was so undone by God's Presence, by His voice! The lies I'd been taught crumbled. All I could say was, "What I believe isn't true. Please reveal Yourself to me."

And in that moment, Jesus ceased to be one of many master teachers. He was not only Savior and Lord, but He was also now *my* Savior and Lord!

It is not unlike God to ask the same question multiple times until we surrender. Jesus asked Peter three times, *"Do you love Me more than these?"* (John 21:15). Each time, the question cut deeper. In Acts 10, Peter had a vision, during which the Lord gave instructions three times before he surrendered and was willing to minister to the Gentiles.

For me, each time God posed the question, lies were exposed, deception shattered, leading me to surrender.

There is only one true and living God. Idols, spirits, and false teachers may try to convince us of their divinity. But only Jesus can save us, transform our lives, give us a new identity, free us, and call us into purpose as He has ordained before the world began. Life is only found in Him. He is God!

A Call to Life and Freedom

If you are reading this, you may sense Holy Spirit tugging at your heart, perhaps even asking you questions about what you believe to be true and challenging you around who or what you serve. He's inviting you to eternal life, a new life that can only be found in Jesus.

Jesus is more than a teacher and a great prophet. He is Savior and LORD, and those who believe in Him have their spiritual DNA changed and take on the very likeness of God.

The Bible describes this as being born again. We are born into the family of God through faith in Jesus Christ! We become children of God.

I hope you are experiencing the presence of Jesus even as you read. If there are areas in your life that need to be surrendered, totally surrender to Him now. Your surrender positions you to experience all God has for you.

If you have never asked Jesus to be your Savior and your Lord, I encourage you to pause and do it right now. This is the most critical decision you will ever make. Allow Jesus to reveal Himself to you; get to know Him in a personal way.

> *...that if you confess with your mouth Jesus as Lord, and believe in your heart that God raised Him from the dead, you will be saved; for with the heart a person believes, resulting in righteousness, and with the mouth he confesses, resulting in salvation.*
> Romans 10:9-10

If you are ready, say this simple prayer aloud: "Dear Lord Jesus, I believe that You died for my sins and rose on the third day. Jesus, come into my heart, live in me, live through me, and live with me. I accept You as my Savior and my LORD. I declare that right now, I am born again. In Jesus' Name!"

CONGRATULATIONS! If you prayed that prayer for the first time, you are born again. Welcome to the family. Use the contact information at the end of this book to reach out to me, and I will be happy to celebrate with you and support you in your relationship with Jesus.

CHAPTER 2

WALKING WITH THE GOD WHOSE NAME I DIDN'T KNOW

Giving my life to Jesus at a spiritualist church convention felt surreal and more than a bit awkward. I didn't tell anyone at first. I knew that people would either question my experience, reinterpret it through a spiritualist's lens, or try to convince me I hadn't heard God's voice. Not only did I not tell anyone, I didn't I run to a Christian church right away. After experiencing so much false teaching, I wasn't sure which churches would teach the truth.

All I knew was that I had embarked on a new, exciting yet a bit scary, journey with God, and if necessary, I'd go it alone.

Academia is Not Enough

I trusted the Bible, God's Word. I trusted His ability to reveal Himself to me through His Word. The Bible became my lifeline, knowing God would enable me to understand the Scripture accurately. He wants all of us to know Him accurately and intimately through the Scripture, with Holy Spirit as our Teacher.

If we approach the Bible academically, we risk becoming overly religious, living by the letter of the Word rather than by the Spirit. If we seek revelation without considering historical and cultural context, we may fall prey to deception and find ourselves drawn to spiritualism and other strange doctrines.

We must consider all of it—the historical, cultural, and the revelatory. We must rely on Holy Spirit to guide us into truth.

When I told my grandmother that I was backing away from Hurley's teachings to study the Bible, she responded as I anticipated.

"The Bible is full of types and shadows," she warned. "You need someone to help you interpret it!" Of course, she meant leaders and teachers from the organization.

Many may get off track, seeking another person to help them understand Scripture without first turning to God Himself. Yes, the Bible is prophetic in nature, with symbols, types, and shadows. We need Holy Spirit to open its meaning to us.

My grandmother's response confirmed that I needed to keep my encounter with God and my study of the Scriptures to myself for a while. The people around me loved me, but they were deceived themselves. No matter how good their intentions, one deceived person cannot free someone until they themselves are free. They could not help me discover a truth they had yet discovered.

Wrong teaching produces wrong belief; wrong beliefs are a catalyst for spiritual experiences and encounters that are not of God. Those encounters reinforce the wrong beliefs and teachings, creating a cycle of bondage that only God can break.

A Season of Separation

There are times when God may lead us into seasons of separation—not isolation— to learn to hear Him more clearly. He did this with the Apostle Paul:

> *But when God, who had set me apart even from my mother's womb and called me through His grace, was pleased to reveal His Son in me so that I might preach Him among the Gentiles, I did not immediately consult with flesh and blood, nor did I go up to Jerusalem to those who were apostles before me; but I went away to Arabia, and returned once more to Damascus.*
> **Galatians 1:15-17**

I entered such a season. I worked, took college classes, worked out, prayed, and studied Scripture. That was it!

My life felt as if it had been turned upside down, and I needed to get a handle on it. I didn't realize it then, but I was grieving. Grieving the wasted years. Grieving the people I'd misled. Grieving the souls that had been deceived, manipulated, and lost because they believed they were loving Jesus when they had really been led away from Him.

I was filled with rage toward George Hurley for deceiving my family and so many others long before I was born.

One day, while I was driving, Holy Spirit said, "*You have to forgive.*"

Unforgiveness would be a hindrance in my walk with God. At first, it seemed strange, even impossible—how do you forgive someone who has passed? But I knew forgiveness was about my freedom. As an act of faith, I said out loud, "I forgive George Hurley for leading my family, me, and others into deception."

Immediately, the weight lifted. I was free.

I thank God for His grace. He would not let me remain angry. He wanted me to live the reality of the covenant I have through Jesus Christ, and forgiveness was a key component.

The Deception of George Hurley

The more I studied, the more I saw how far George Hurley had fallen. A gifted young Baptist preacher, who as a child, preached to the trees, grew hungry for more of God—a hunger I believe came from God, who uses hunger as an invitation to know Him more intimately. Unfortunately, instead of pressing deeper into God's Word, Hurley turned to the occult, studying under well-known occult masters. He traveled to Asia and Egypt, where he was taught counterfeit wisdom, returning to the U.S. with doctrines of demons.

Hurley's exposure to the occult opened him to deceptive visions. After long suffering, fasting, praying, and studying, he considered himself worthy to be ordained as the prophet and "Christ" of the Aquarian Age.

Deception mimics the real. Hurley structured the organization's "church" much like a traditional denominational church, blending the occult with the Word of God. They even sang church hymns, replacing the name of Jesus with Hurley's name.

Cultivating Intimacy with God

I share these details to point out the tragedy of failing to discern God's voice. Despite his Christian roots, Hurley was led astray because he failed to discern the voice of God and isolated himself from the community of true believers and godly counsel. Isolation is dangerous.

> *He who separates himself seeks his own desire, He*
> *quarrels against all sound wisdom.*
> **Proverbs 18:1**

Some enter times of isolation, believing they were in a season of separation to receive revelation from God. Isolation often becomes a place that breeds deception.

Positions, titles, and platforms do not guarantee a relationship with God. Simply studying the historical context of Scripture does not guarantee a relationship with God. Gifts do not guarantee a relationship with God. Intimacy with Holy Spirit, Scripture study, heartfelt devotion, and an openness to revelation help us truly know God's voice.

Our spirits came from God. We were created to know His voice! Cultivating intimacy with Him increases our sensitivity to His voice. As we come to know God's voice and follow Him, He will use us in tremendous ways to positively impact the lives of others, some of whom we may never meet.

And our own lives will be better than we could ever imagine as we live out His purposes for us. This is not to say our lives will be without challenges, but in the middle of those challenges, we can have peace and joy knowing that God is with us and has already given us the victory in Jesus.

Calling Him by Name

As I studied the Bible, beginning with Genesis, I was intentional in my approach. I read slowly, prayerfully, inviting Holy Spirit, the Teacher, to speak to me.

During my studies, I encountered the name Jehovah and began to call God by that name. The name Jehovah does not appear explicitly in the Bible until Genesis 22:14, when Abraham named a place "Jehovah Jireh," meaning "The LORD provides." However, we do see the word "LORD" —the English equivalent of the Hebrew name Yahweh— in Genesis 2:4.

At first, I wasn't confident or comfortable saying, "Jesus," even though I had given my life to Him. In the organization, Jesus was not seen as *the* Christ, but only as *a* Christ, one among many enlightened masters. They believe there are seven spirits or levels to reach Christ's level of enlightenment. They also taught that there is a new Christ for every astrological age.

Side note: Unfortunately, some Christians believe astrology is innocent, but it is not. It is idolatry in disguise; each sign represents a spirit. When an individual submits to an astrological sign, they submit to the nature and characteristics of that spirit, coming under the lordship of the spirit the sign represents.

Even joking about being under an astrological sign is dangerous. The words we speak can either produce life or death. They grant access to God or to the demonic realm. There is no in-between, no neutral ground. The spiritual impact of words is not ignored simply because they were spoken harmlessly, jokingly, or in ignorance.

> ***Death and life are in the power of the tongue, And those who love it will eat its fruit.***
> **Proverbs 18:21**

To Know Him as He Is

Yes, I knew Jesus was *the* Christ, but I still had to unlearn false teaching. I had to know Him as He is, not as others had presented Him to me. Some spiritualists and mediums called Him Master Jesus, but never as LORD, and never as Savior.

Satan has always tried to make people question Jesus' identity (Luke 4:3). As a result, the person may only see Jesus as a prophet or master teacher who is no different from Buddha, Mohammed, or any other teacher esteemed in other religions or spiritual beliefs. But Jesus' deity, virgin birth, cross, and resurrection are not symbolic—they are reality.

Getting to know Jesus as Lord and Savior was a new experience for me. I learned about the name Jehovah (Yahweh), which is the personal name of God. And, because God reveals His nature and attributes through His name, I began studying His other names. I discovered the various names associated with Jehovah, such as Jehovah-Raphe (The LORD Who Heals) and Jehovah-shalom (The LORD, My Peace).

Supernatural Encounters with Jesus

One night, I was spending time with Him before going to bed. I knelt by my bed, eyes closed, face pressed into the mattress; the lights were off, the blinds were closed. The room was completely dark.

When I ended my prayer time and opened my eyes, a bright light filled the room. I just stared, amazed.

Soon, the bright light began to resemble a ball or orb. It hovered in the middle of the room for a few minutes, then disappeared. I knew this was a manifest presence of God.

Another time, I was praying in my bedroom…the same posture as before. This time, the light was on. When I finished praying, I got up to turn off the light. I hit the switch, but the room remained brightly lit. I turned the light back on; the brightness of the room remained the same. I turned the light off again. Nothing changed.

After doing this several times, I realized that it was the visible, tangible Presence of God, the manifestation of His glory, that remained. I thought, "Cool!" and went to bed.

If I'd known then what I know now, I would have lingered in His Presence. When we spend time with God, we must pause—listen, soak, and allow Him to work in our spirits. Not every moment with Him is about speaking or decreeing; sometimes it's simply about being with Him. This time together is often about an exchange. We must savor time with Holy Spirit and value each moment we spend with Him. The more time we spend with Him, the more we develop a heightened sensitivity to His ever-dwelling Presence with and in us.

Powerful encounters like these allowed me to discard the mediumship items I still had, even though I no longer used them. I felt a sense of freedom as I realized I didn't need anything. I needed only the proper heart posture and His Word to commune with God.

I'd been taught that I needed a wooden altar raised on glass, with candles, incense, and precise times of meditation facing East—rigid rituals to commune with the spirit. It involved a significant amount of effort and work.

In Christ, I discovered freedom. I could simply talk to Jehovah, knowing He not only heard me but would also respond.

God desires to commune with you; you don't need objects or formulas. All you need is the proper heart posture and desire to be with Him. He will respond.

Growing in His Name

As I continued to study and encounter Jesus, my discomfort with His name disappeared. I learned the power of praying in Jesus' name, not to other spirits.

> *Whatever you ask in My name, that will I do, so that the Father may be glorified in the Son. If you ask Me anything in My name, I will do it.*
> John 14:13-14

God taught me the reality of the Trinity—one God who reveals Himself as Father, Son (The Word), and Holy Spirit. This revelation helped me to unlearn what I was taught about every spirit, except evil ones, being part of God, and that all people are "God within" and all are connected to God.

Our spirits did come from God. Because of that, we long for connection with Him because eternity has been placed in our hearts (Ecclesiastes 3:11).

Our spirits are of eternal substance and have been placed within the soul, and both have been placed within a body. We are three-part beings, just like God. In our spirit form, we are not God. We are made in His image, according to His likeness (Genesis 1:26-27), functioning as "gods" (*elohims*) in the Earth (Psalm 82:6), *but we are not God*. We were created; God was not.

After becoming comfortable with calling God by His name, I

had to learn about the authority I have as a believer through His name. Leaving the organization caused me to experience a season of intense spiritual warfare, as anyone who leaves the occult or the new age does. I had to learn how to war as a believer

God graciously gave me a time of peace and preparation before war.

Chapter 3

Darkness Masquerades as Light

In those days before I encountered Jesus and surrendered to Him, spiritual experiences were my normal. I thought they were holy, powerful, and proof that I was walking with God. Now, I see them for what they really were—counterfeits.

Protected?

"I have your picture on my altar."

I heard that phrase more times than I can count within the organization. It meant someone was sending spirits against another to control, stop, or harm them. Mediums didn't always get along with each other; some competed for status, jealous of another's abilities. When one master medium could do something another couldn't, they would accuse that medium of showing off.

I was in high school when my mother told me that she was in a "psychic war." Another spiritualist within the city was trying to send spirits to her.

"Don't go to that part of the city. I cannot protect you there!" she warned.

She made a talisman for me to carry in my wallet to protect me from evil spirits, possibly sent to harm me. I didn't know enough to protect myself at the time, so I did exactly as she told me.

The Battle for My Soul

One night, lying in bed, I saw a red light and a tall dark figure wearing a top hat, holding a thick wand. I thought I was dreaming, but when I opened my eyes, the figure kept coming until it stood beside me. Then it struck me with the wand.

"What are you doing?" I shouted.

The figure backed into the red light and vanished.

The next day, I told my mother what had happened.

"Let's pray that the spirit did not accomplish what it was sent to do," she said.

Another time, I was lying in my bed, and a spirit appeared in the form of my deceased uncle. The spirit lifted me off the bed, laughing, as I squirmed

"Put me down!" I demanded.

The spirit continued laughing and smirked at me for a few minutes before finally putting me down and disappearing.

My family told me my uncle's spirit was playing a joke on me. I didn't think it was funny. I now realize that this spirit was not my uncle's; it was a familiar spirit disguised as my uncle to trick me into trusting it.

That's how deception works. Familiar spirits are not angels; they are not sent from God. They are demonic spirits, assigned by Satan to people and their families. They become familiar with those they are assigned to by watching their tendencies and behaviors.

They learn the person's likes and dislikes and listen to what they say if they have access. They also try to appear as a relative who has transitioned or someone the individual respects to gain that person's trust. I had been taught about familiar spirits in the organization, but was told they were "kind" spirits because they spoke nicely and appeared to be loving.

The Power of Music

My mother, a gifted pianist and organist, often recorded the musical expressions of our "worship" gatherings. One service the people were in "high praise"—clapping, singing, beating tambourines. The musicians were playing "shouting music," as the people lifted up the name of George Hurley in song. Nothing out of the ordinary.

After the service, my mother played her recording. "Jamal, come, listen to this!" she called excitedly. As I listened to the recording with her, I could hear various swishing sounds, like wind, layered in the music—some soft, some aggressive. Some seemed closer than others. The sound overshadowed the music, which could be heard faintly in the background. We had captured the sound of the active spirits during the service.

My mother asked others who had also recorded if they had heard anything on their recordings; they had not. We thought it was a special for us to have captured those sounds. I now realize that it was God's grace, opening my spiritual ears, allowing recognize the sounds of demonic activity hidden in music

Evil spirits respond to and use music as a means of entry into people's lives. What we sing or allow to enter our souls through music will invite either the Spirit of God or spirits of darkness. These evil spirits were highly active as expressions of worship were released to a spiritual principality disguised as George Hurley, or rather, the spiritual principality that he served. When a person follows the teachings or doctrine of a person, they submit to the spirit that influences that person. You must be careful who and what you listen to.

True Worship Ascends

As believers, we cannot approach the expressions of worship through music at our gatherings casually. Music is not limited to what many have categorized as praise and worship. Music inspired by and directed toward God is an *expression* of worship.

When expressions of worship are released, God responds, and so do His angels (Psalm 22:3). The sound released through music does something in three dimensions. First, it releases God's Presence and causes angelic movement in the Earth. It echoes in Heaven, and all who dwell there add their expressions as it goes before the throne of God the Father. It causes demons to tremble and experience torment. Depending on the sound, the music is used as a weapon of warfare (2 Chronicles 20:21-22).

We must be confident in what is happening in the realm of the spirit during expressions of worship to Jesus. We must never just offer music that entertains, sounds good, or focuses on us. If we do, we will only get the attention of people and miss what God desires to do.

Jesus shared this principle in Matthew 6 when He spoke about praying and giving to the poor. If we do either to gain attenton, that is our only reward—being seen by men. What we do from a sincere heart toward God will be rewarded by God openly. We should always remember that during times of worship through music, we are interacting with a Holy God in the presence of people.

The Touch Lamp

During my senior year of high school, I lived with my grandmother. In my room, which had been my uncle's room, there was a light switch on the wall near the door controlled the ceiling light, and on a long, heavy dresser were two touch lamps, one on each end, that turned on and off by touching the base.

Often when my grandmother or I returned home after dark, the touch lamps and other lights throughout the house would be on, though neither of us had turned them on before we left. It never frighten us because we'd grown used to supernatural activity.

"Your uncle's spirit turned the lights on for me," my grandmother would say. I believed his spirit was guiding and helping us.

One day, I conducted a test. I put school textbook on the base of one of the lamps; nothing happened. I drummed on the base with pencils—boom, tat, boom, boom, tat—nothing happened. I did a drum roll with ink pens, imitating the drummers from school, still nothing.

The only time the lamp came on was when I touched it.

One night, while I was lying in bed with the lights off, the touch lamp suddenly came on. I felt a rush of excitement; this was proof a spirit was indeed turning it on.

"Yes!" I thought to myself.

Then the rush shifted, I wanted to run out of the room. Even though I was used to this kind of activity, I felt fear.

"Don't be scared, Jamal," I told myself.

I would not allow myself to fear a spirit making itself known to me. I knew I could not engage in the spiritual realm if I were fearful.

I Saw a Spirit Enter Me

My grandmother "pastored" a congregation at a small, three-leveled building in Pontiac. My mother was a skilled musician, and when I was a young child, I would sit on her lap while she played the piano. She would tell me to press the black keys while she played the white keys.

She played the piano in the weekly services; another musician played the organ. After the organist left, my mother became the lead musician, playing the organ, while I played the trumpet.

I dabbled on the piano, and when my mother received another assignment at a different location, I assumed the role of lead musician.

My grandmother gave me a key to the building so I could practice as often as I wanted. Every time I entered the building alone, I would rush to turn on the lights because I could feel a strong presence. I always made sure to leave before dark. I did not like locking up the building at night alone because of that same presence.

One day, while practicing, I started playing "shouting" music. A dark figure appeared near the doors. It took three strides toward me and entered my body.

I shook uncontrollably for a couple of minutes. Once the shaking stopped, I could barely play at all; my coordination was off. Unable to continue, I left. I told no one.

Riding in a Car Made Invisible

My mother and cousin, Cherri, were attending a convention at the national headquarters in Detroit. My mother had just launched a location in Sarnia, Canada. Because it was new and people had just started to attend consistently, she did not want to cancel the service. We left Detroit heading to Sarnia, approximately an hour and a half away.

We didn't have much time and needed to get there as quickly as possible. Cherri, an intense and aggressive driver, drove; my mother sat in the passenger side of the front seat; I was in the back.

Cars swerved and cut in front of us, almost hitting us, as if they didn't see us. Several cars next to us attempted to enter our lane.

Cherri yelled, "Pay attention!" She honked the car horn. The drivers appeared startled.

"It's OK," my mother said calmly. "They can't see you."

Then it happened again. A driver in the car right next to us attempted to enter our lane. Cherri swerved out of the way, honked the horn, and yelled, "Watch it, idiot!"

My mother said again, a little louder, "It's OK. They can't see you."

"What?" Cherri was confused.

"They can't see you because we are invisible to them," my mother said plainly. She meant it literally.

Master-level mediums commonly became invisible. They physically stepped into the spiritual realm, unseen in the natural realm, even though they were still present in the spirit.

Cherri took a few seconds to process it, then responded, "Oh, OK," and continued driving.

How were we invisible? Was it really possible? But the look of shock on the other drivers' faces seemed to confirm it.

I thought it would be cool to learn how to become invisible.

Learning to Live in and from His Presence

Back then, these experiences felt normal. The more I invited them to be a part of my life, the more my sensitivity to them increased. The more sensitive I become, the more active the spirits became. They showed up more, spoke more, used me more.

Those spirits desired to be a part of my life, to teach me, and to reveal things for me to share with others. Since I thought what I was doing was of God, I wanted the same. That's how deception works; it lures you. You will passionately pursue them, giving permission to more ungodly, demonic spiritual activity to occur. The increase in activity deepens the deception, and the person becomes trapped in a cycle until they encounter Jesus in a powerful way.

The domain of darkness imitates the Kingdom of God and how Holy Spirit works in the lives of believers. Holy Spirit desires to be a part of our daily lives. He desires to engage with us at a high level, to speak to us, to inhabit our spirits, impacting our souls, and resting on our physical bodies.

Unfortunately, some have reduced their experience of Holy Spirit to a feeling. They refer to Him as "it." Others say they "caught" the Holy Ghost based on a physical response to a song or sermon. Holy Spirit is not an "it" or a feeling. He is God, the Spirit of Truth. He is not an "it" that we catch; He is a Person we walk with.

We cannot reduce our time communing with Him to a feeling or a physical response. We must also not reduce our relationship with Him to our prayer times or the expression of the gifts He demonstrates through us. He cannot be limited to 30 minutes, 60 minutes, or 2 hours of prayer. He is not limited to miracles, signs, wonders, prophecy, healings, casting out demons, and so on.

While all these things are important, we must realize that Holy Spirit is the Spirit of God and is greater than all those things.

It is essential that we increase our sensitivity to His Presence, to His voice, and allow Him to reveal Himself to us. We must spend time with God and live in a perpetual place of awareness of His Presence while intentionally stewarding that Presence. This involves striking a delicate balance between interacting with God through His Word and His Presence.

Many focus on Presence but are not rooted in the Word. That may cause them to be sensitive to the movement of Holy Spirit, but lack the revelation necessary to live their lives in accordance with what they have experienced. When we do that, we move from encounter to encounter without reaching maturity.

Believers who focus strictly on the Word without experiencing Presence risk becoming legalistic, religious, and insensitive to the movement of God. They have knowledge of the Word, but lack the revelation necessary to discern what God is saying and doing in the moment.

God is a Spirit, and He is the Word.

> *God is a Spirit: and they that worship him must*
> *worship him in spirit and in truth.*
> John 4:24 (KJV)

> *In the beginning was the Word, and the Word was*
> *with God, and the Word was God.*
> John 1:1 (KJV)

As we approach God properly, we cultivate deeper levels of intimacy with Him. Out of this place of intimacy, our gifts develop, and Holy Spirit will use us in supernatural ways to demonstrate

His love, power, and Presence to others so they can come to know Jesus as Savior and Lord.

Supernatural experiences with, in, and by Holy Spirit are and can be our normal. We do not have to wait for a worship gathering to experience God in the ways He desires us to experience Him. The Presence of Holy Spirit is not just for us to simply recognize when He's doing something; it is for us to live in and from. We have the privilege of being able to do life with God, experiencing Him in real and tangible ways every day.

I believe the days are gone when it was rare to have supernatural experiences with God. In the Body of Christ, we have allowed these things to become so rare that when they do happen, we celebrate them as a special occasion and limit them to just that one experience. Then, we attempt to develop formulas to facilitate supernatural occurrences. While every encounter with God is extraordinary, they are meant to be normal for the believer; the supernatural cannot be formulated.

It is time for the Body of Christ to return to a place of normalcy, experiencing the power and Presence of God where we truly live on Earth as we will in Heaven.

CHAPTER 4

PREPARING FOR WAR

"I'm going to see my girl today—I need a favor," my friend, Tim said. "Her friend, Valerie, is visiting her. I need you to come and keep her friend occupied so I can have Lacy's undivided attention."

I agreed to help him out, and Tim let Lacy know I was coming with him.

"He can come," Valerie said, "but he better not think he's gonna holla." This woman didn't know me and was already giving attitude.

"I'm not going," I told Tim at his house as he prepared to leave. He'd changed outfits several times and had to ensure he wore the right cologne. I typically would have done the same, but it didn't matter. I had no intentions of going with him.

"I'm not going, man," I said.

I stood firm—until something I still can't explain happened.

"I'm not..." but by the time I got the word "going" out, I was sitting in the passenger seat of Tim's car, 15 minutes away from his house. One moment, I was standing in his living room, the next I was in the car.

I stared out the car window, thinking, "What...just... happened?"

No turning back now.

"This is Who I Have for You"
We arrived at Lacy's apartment. When she opened the door, I immediately saw a bright golden light—God's glory. Then, I had a vision of Valerie sitting on the couch. I heard the voice of God say, "*This is who I have for you.*"

"OK," I replied, and the vision ended.

Inside the apartment, Valerie was sitting where I'd seen her. I was confident—maybe too confident. I just knew I'd be leaving with her phone number; she'd be my woman from that day forward. After all, I had heard from the LORD.

It didn't work that way.

I believed she was my woman from that day forward because I believed I had what God had spoken. But I was overconfident, got in the flesh, and almost messed it up with the second sentence I spoke.

When we receive a Word from God, we should be confident, but we must also use wisdom as well. We must allow God to bring to pass His Word in His way. That day was orchestrated so I'd have to rely on Him. I wasn't dressed to impress. No cologne, no props, no externals. My confidence had to be in God alone.

We had a great time. The next logical step for me was to get Valerie's phone number. I asked; she said no. I was shocked. Didn't she know what God had said? To recover from feeling dismissed, I gave her my number.

She did not call me until two weeks later…when Holy Spirit directed her to.

Surrendering the Search

Before meeting Valerie, I'd tried to find the "right" woman. No one, no matter what they had going for them, was *the one*. A medium from the organization sent me a message saying "the spirit" wanted me to date his daughter. I knew that wasn't God.

A week before meeting Valerie, having become increasingly frustrated, I committed to focusing solely on my relationship with God. I surrendered my search, and God orchestrated the right connection.

God used Val to support me so I would not feel alone as I walked through the warfare I experienced. He also used her to lead me to Word of Life, where I eventually became a member and remained until we relocated to Cincinnati, Ohio.

Word of Life

I wouldn't have found the worship fellowship God wanted me to be a part of on my own. I may have picked a "good" one, but I may not have received all God had for me in that season. We have to allow Holy Spirit to led us.

As Valerie and I got to know each other, I saw her commitment to serving in the church as a worship leader. One Sunday, Holy Spirit said, "Follow her to church."

So I drove to her house, and I *literally* followed her to church. (In hindsight, I realize we could have ridden together and perhaps I wouldn't have seemed like a stalker. When God gives us direction, clarity matters).

One of the assistant pastors taught that day, and I really don't remember much of the message. It was the time of the musical expression of worship that struck me. I watched as everyone, hands raised, voices lifted in song, truly engaged with God! I felt uncomfortable; I'd never witnessed such intentionality. They sought an encounter with the LORD, and that focus was strangely new to me.

You Saw Me?

The first time I met the pastor of Word of Life, Valerie had gone to borrow some resources from him to complete an assignment for a class she was taking. As we pulled up, the pastor came out carrying a stack of Bible dictionaries, encyclopedias, and commentaries.

"Can you wait a moment?" he asked, after putting the books in the back seat.

He disappeared into the church and returned a few minutes later with more books. This man studied the Scripture in depth! That dedication to the Word earned him my respect, and motivated me to visit the church the following Sunday to hear him teach.

On that second visit, I thought I'd go undercover, like Nicodemus had done with Jesus (John 3:1-2). To be inconspicuous, I thought I'd "cloak" myself, using the spiritual practice of invisibility. And though I was no longer a medium, and despite never having done it before, I somehow thought I could get away with it.

What was I thinking? You cannot take spiritualist teachings and practices and apply them to Jesus—this unholy mixing. Besides, those spirits were not going to help me hear the Word of God!

I sat in the back of the church, and listened. I loved the whole worship experience.

When I got home, Valerie called.

"I saw you at church," she said. "Why didn't you speak to me?"

"You saw me?" I responded in surprise.

"Yes, I saw you!"

"I thought I was invisible."

Valerie laughed hysterically for what seemed like an eternity. She still laughs every time she recalls that conversation.

Planted

From then on, I was planted at Word of Life.

The rumors spread.

"He left spiritualism and became a Christian because of Valerie. He's so infatuated with her that he 'changed gods.'"

"He's whipped," they said. "A skirt-chaser."

Others claimed I'd had a tantrum after a disagreement with my grandmother and left.

None of that was true.

The LORD planted me at Word of Life. We must be where God wants us to be to experience all He has for us. Fulfilling God's call on our lives is contingent on *where* we are fed and *what* you are fed. It matters where you receive the Word.

Being connected to a worship fellowship is about spiritual growth and community, both essential as we fulfill our purposes and destiny. God led me to a place where I began to learn about faith and how to apply its principles while witnessing the demonstration of His power.

God-Led, Not Emotion-Led

As I mentioned, some believed I'd left the organization out of anger. I have learned not to be led by emotions, but only by the Spirit of God. I have also learned the importance of covenant.

Disagreements should never break covenant relationships unless absolutely necessary. Too often, people make decisions rooted in emotion, based on circumstances: divorce or separation, career, church, and city. Decisions based on emotions alone usually don't lead us in the right direction, the direction God desires. Emotions change based on perspective.

As we learn to walk together in community as God designed, misunderstandings are inevitable. If we bolt or sever a God-ordained relationship, we may leave the very place where God has planted us to mature and equip us.

This is true of any area of our lives, and especially, when we leave a place the wrong way. We take all the soul wounds that were never addressed and a skewed perspective to the next place. How we leave a place sets the stage for how we enter the next place. Believers should not "church hop." We must discern the difference between our emotions and the Spirit of God. We only transition when He leads us.

Offense is a weapon the enemy uses against us to move us out of place. That weapon did not work on me, nor did reverse psychology. Don't allow the adversary to use it to deceive you.

The Inevitability of War

Things were exciting. God was revealing Himself to me while I simultaneously experienced intense spiritual warfare. The warfare I experienced as a believer differed from the warfare I experienced as a spiritualist.

Many who have experienced the type of spiritual warfare I have (which I share in more detail in the next chapter) do not discuss it out of fear of being misunderstood or called crazy. I had those thoughts and feelings also, and for that reason, I remained silent. I have only recently begun sharing those experiences with others to help them.

I talked to one person during that time—Valerie. I knew I could trust her. God ordered my steps and used Valerie to guide me to where I needed to be, when I needed it, to receive the revelation I required. Often, what you need for your breakthrough is found in the community of mature believers.

CHAPTER 5

FIGHTING FROM VICTORY

As I began walking closer with God, the warfare intensified. Demons, who appeared as dark, shadowy figures—some with long talon-like nails—began to manifest in physical form at night, attacking me as I slept. These weren't nightmares, but tangible, visible and violent attacks in both the physical realm and my dream state.

Even though I had given my life to Jesus and was attending a church, I often felt defenseless. I didn't know how to make the attacks stop. I loved God, spent time with Him, He spoke to me daily. But I hadn't learned my authority as a believer. I didn't know how to stand in what He had already given me.

Power in the Name

One Sunday, I attended a class at Word of Life on *The Believer's Authority,* a book by Kenneth Hagin, Sr. The revelation in that book was exactly what I needed. God was answering my prayer and equipping me with the very weapon I needed to end the onslaught of attacks. Hungry, desperate and determined, I devoured the book in one day.

That night, three demons appeared as usual. Having knowledge about the authority I had in Jesus did not stop them from attacking; exercising that authority did. I was armed with the revelation of God's power in the name of Jesus, and I was ready. I rebuked them in the name of Jesus, and they fled immediately.

I slept soundly for the first time in weeks.

The next night, they came again. Again, I rebuked them in the name of Jesus. Again, they fled.

On next night, they returned, but with a fourth demon who had four arms. Before I could say anything, it grabbed me from behind, restraining me with three of its arms as I struggled to get loose. With the fourth arm, it covered my mouth with its thick, nasty fingers to keep me from saying the name "Jesus."

I shook my head wildly until I could breathe out one word: "Jesus!"

All four demons left, and never attacked me in that way again. When we operate in revelation from God, things change.

Why Had God Allowed It?

You might wonder why God didn't simply stop the demons from attacking me. Why would He allow that to happen? He could have prevented the attacks; He could have allowed my angels to fight for me, but He didn't. He *wanted* me to fight. Some lessons can't be learned by observation.

God used that experience to teach me how to operate in His authority. Based on His call on my life, He knew I needed to learn how to exercise His authority over evil spirits and teach others how to do the same. That experience prepared me for the ministry He called me to.

God does some things sovereignly, and accomplishes other things in partnership with us. Now, no demon can manifest and attack me physically or in a dream. I've learned to live from and stand in the revelation that I learned back then.

I have learned the authority I have in the Name above all names—Jesus.

Reverencing His Name

It is essential that we reverence the name of Jesus. Far too often, people use His name casually, or even as profanity, not realizing the power and authority in His name. They do not realize there is power in the name Jesus.

We must recognize that power. Acts 4:12 tells us:

> ***And there is salvation in no one else; for there is
> no other name under heaven that has been given
> among mankind by which we must be saved."***

That word salvation doesn't just refer to going to Heaven when we transition from Earth. Salvation includes preservation, deliverance, and healing. Jesus is the only name that preserves us, delivers us, heals us. The Name enables God's government to be demonstrated in Earth as it is in Heaven. When we understand this reality, we will stop using His name lightly, and use it as Scripture instructs We will recognize the holiness of the name Jesus and reverence it.

If you have left the new age, the occult, spiritualism, or religion, and are having similar experiences, I encourage you to study what the Scripture says about your authority as a believer and the power of the name Jesus. Exercise it! You are not powerless!

Learn who Jesus is, who He is in you, who you are in Him, and be free!

They Kept Coming Back

After the nightly attacks ended, I was charged and ready to fight. I anointed my apartment with oil, prayed in tongues, and commanded every demon to leave. I actually saw them run out—but they kept coming back.

Confused, I asked, "Holy Spirit, why are the demons allowed to come back after I commanded them to leave and not return?"

One evening, He opened my eyes. I sat in the living room watching television with Cherri. I saw angels standing on one side of the room and demons on the other, facing them. The demons couldn't act because of God's angels. However, the angels did not kick the demons out.

Holy Spirit explained: the lease for the apartment listed both my name and Cherri's. When I exercised my authority, the demons had to obey me. However, when Cherri engaged in spiritualist practices, they had legal right to return. Because Jesus was the highest authority, even though they returned, the demons were powerless.

Holy Spirit showed me my jurisdiction. In my bedroom, I had full authority; they could not enter. In Cherri's room, she had authority. In shared spaces—the kitchen, bathroom, and living room—the demons could stand, but not operate. They were bound by the presence of God that was with me.

I was grateful for the revelation; it freed me. I stopped wasting time fighting something that had legal permission to remain.

Until I moved, I didn't spend much time in the apartment; I was there when I needed to rest, staying in my room. I often wondered how my behavior at that time impacted my relationship with Cherri.

Don't Fight the Chicken Grease

Shortly after that, I'd notice a single drop of oil in the center of the stove—always in the same spot. Since I'd anointed the apartment, I thought Cherri had also anointed it. I'd wiped up the oil and declared, *"No weapon formed against me will prosper,"* each time I saw it.

By the fourth day, I was irritated.

One morning, as I prepared breakfast, I saw, out of the corner of my eye, oil dripping from the vent above the stove. It slowly dripped to the same spot, and I realized grease had lodged in the small vents. Cherri had fried chicken earlier that week, and some grease must have splattered on the fan.

What I thought was a spiritual act against me was simply splattered chicken grease.

Not everything is a demon!

We cannot become superstitious. Spiritual warfare often puts us on high alert, but that must not lead us to superstition. To believe that every negative thing is demonic activity is bondage. Some things are simply the result of human error, or life itself.

We must be aware, but we should not in live constant fight mode. That invites stress to the soul and the body, producing adverse mental and physical conditions.

Even though I had been dealing with spiritual warfare, everything was not the result of that warfare. Cherri wasn't doing anything. I was fighting, thinking I was in another stage of a spiritual battle when there was no battle at all. I thought everything was an attack.

The Scripture admonishes us that, because we desire to live righteously, we will experience persecution (2 Timothy 3:12 NASB). This persecution may come in different forms. We must be sober-minded and first be willing to assess rather than assume.

Don't fight the chicken grease.

CHAPTER 6

SPIRITUAL WARFARE CONTINUES

"Renounce the spirit of George Hurley," Holy Spirit instructed.

I'd learned about the name and blood of Jesus, but "renouncing" was new to me. I had already confessed Jesus, thrown out all the organization's materials, and left that world behind. Still, the Lord asked for a formal break—a spoken cut-off.

Salvation of the Soul: Renounce

I'd done all I knew to do and thought that had been sufficient. Now, Holy Spirit was requiring me to do something I had no knowledge of. What did it mean to renounce something? I trusted Holy Spirit to help me understand what He was requiring of me.

To renounce is "to give up something by formal declaration." Our words have the power to produce life or death (Proverbs 18:21). Because of my relationship with Jesus, some things that had been produced in the spiritual realm no longer had power over me. However, they still needed to be dismantled by faith through declaration. Entry points still remained, and they needed to be cut off.

> *"You will also decree a thing, and it will be estab-*
> *lished for you; And light will shine on your ways.*
> **Job 22:28**

When we make a decree, we establish or enforce spiritual law in the Earth. Only believers have the authority to make a decree and establish spiritual law. However, every person—believer or unbeliever—can release life or death through their words.

Producing death through words is often referred to as a word curse. Those who engage in witchcraft use words to cast spells and perform incantations. Spiritualists use words to control spirits and accomplish their desires. We must not underestimate the significance of our words. Jesus made it clear: we will answer for every idle, unproductive word that we say (Matthew 12:36).

I wasn't dealing with Hurley's spirit, but the demonic principality that had motivated him, worked through him, and deceived many. And though I didn't full understand, I obeyed. A complete understanding is not required; faith is.

"In the name of Jesus, I renounce the spirit of George Hurley and Cassie Bell Hurley. You have no right to me, my life, or anything that pertains to me! In Jesus' Name!"

I immediately felt nauseated and began to sweat profusely. I ran to the bathroom and started vomiting. For several days, all I could do was lie in bed or on the couch, too weak to move. I only drank water or ginger ale to soothe my stomach. I'm rarely sick, and thought I was dealing with some virus. I later realized my body was responding to the uprooting of something demonic in my soul.

Salvation of the Soul: Remove

We must be sensitive to Holy Spirit when He reveals that something in our souls may need uprooting. Our spirits are perfect, made whole the moment we accept Jesus as Savior and Lord. However, some things in the soul—our mind, will, emotions, appetites, and desires— must be worked out. The method God uses is based on how deeply things are rooted.

Our soul, unlike our spirit, is the place where our thoughts are managed. We do not think from our physical brains; the physical brain only processes thoughts and sends them through the body as electricity. We think in the soul realm, which is why we do not want it contaminated.

Holy Spirit may be speaking to you as you read, revealing something in your soul that needs to be removed. I encourage you to allow Him to help you in this moment. Say this simple prayer: "Father, in the name of Jesus, I loose from my soul..." Now speak whatever Holy Spirit has revealed to you.

After you pray that prayer, wait a few minutes and allow Holy Spirit to work. Once you sense He has completely loosed those things from your soul, say, "Father, in the name of Jesus, I attach to my soul Your love, peace, joy…" Then, say what Holy Spirit revealed to you that needs to be deposited into your soul.

Salvation of the Soul: Replace

It is essential that after you remove something, you replace it with something of godly substance to prevent that area from being empty. Any area of the soul left empty is open for demon spirits to come and replant things. Jesus said:

> *"Now when the unclean spirit goes out of a man, it passes through waterless places seeking rest, and does not find it. Then it says, 'I will return to my house from which I came'; and when it comes, it finds it unoccupied, swept, and put in order. Then it goes and takes along with it seven other spirits more wicked than itself, and they go in and live there; and the last state of that man becomes worse than the first. That is the way it will also be with this evil generation."*
> Matthew 12:43-45

This principle applies to things that have been planted in the soul. Many people make the mistake of attempting to get themselves together *before* they come to Jesus. This is a deceptive trick of the enemy. The reality is that once we come to Jesus, He helps us to get ourselves together. This is the process of having things uprooted from our soul, healing it, and restoring it.

Evicted

I knew I couldn't remain in the apartment I shared with my cousin because of the evil spirits she invited. She didn't understand the effect of her practices. I only recognized it after I came to Jesus and saw the difference between God's His Kingdom of light and the imitation.

During that time, I often attended prayer gatherings either at the church or in someone's home. Praying with the community of believers strengthens us. During one of those gatherings, a woman prophesied that I would be put out of my apartment. "Don't worry," she encouraged, "God has already made provision."

How could I be put out? My name was on the lease and our rent current?

A week later, while I was in my room, Cherri burst in, shouting, "Stop praying in the name of Jesus! Prayer doesn't do…" And she used a few choice words.

The argument escalated, partly because of my immaturity.

"GET OUT!" I yelled and I pushed her. I tried to close the door, but she angrily pushed back.

"You squished my arm!" she protested. "You have to leave!"

"I'm not going anywhere! My name was on the lease."

I managed to close the door; I needed to put some space between us.

She stood in the hallway, yelling, "Get out now!"

I called another relative, Terry, and told him what had happened, hoping he could calm the situation. I discovered that Cherri had informed the leasing office that I was moving out. My name had been removed from the lease.

I called Valerie and told her what had happened. A few minutes after we hung up, she called back. "My mother said you can come stay with her for a short time."

Provision had been made. The prophetic word came to pass.

But I was hurt and confused. How could my cousin just put me out? I now know it wasn't her, but the spirits she entertained. I couldn't see that then.

Seeing from the Kingdom Perspective

I had to process my feelings before God could reveal that to me. It's vital, even in the middle of processing events and the accompanying emotions, that we remain sensitive to hear the voice of God.

Hearing His voice as He reveals what is really happening helps us see things from a higher perspective—a Kingdom perspective. The peace that follows enables us to process those events more effectively.

At first I felt humiliated. I was engaged, in college, with child to care for. Now I was sleeping on my future mother-in-law's couch. It wasn't supposed to be like that.

I wondered if Valerie thought less of me; I did. All my past friendships were gone, close relationships were gone, primarily because I'd given my life to Jesus. And even though I was forming new relationships, I felt alone

I knew my future was bright, and I would accomplish my childhood dreams, but my present reality seemed to be a stark contradiction. Heaviness and despair had enveloped me. Thank God that He pulled me out of that place as I sat on Val's mother's couch.

We must face our emotions. Many psychologists suggest that we need to allow ourselves to "feel" and advise us to sit with those emotions. Yes, we need to allow ourselves to feel; ignoring our feelings under the guise of operating in faith is a mistake. Faith does not ignore; it supersedes. While acknowledging our emotions, we must not allow ourselves to go to a place of heaviness and despair. That can cause soul wounds. Wounded souls impact our relationship with God and others.

God gives us beauty for ashes and the oil of joy for mourning (Isaiah 61:3). He gave us emotions; they enhance our experiences and enrich our lives. But we must master them, refusing to allow them to take us into mentally or physically unhealthy places. When we learn to live from the joy of the Lord, He is glorified.

Comforted by the Word

God pulled me from a place of despair through a phone call from Valerie. She encouraged me and sent me scriptures.

> *Blessed are those who have been persecuted for the sake of righteousness, for theirs is the kingdom of heaven.*

> *Blessed are you when people insult you and persecute you, and falsely say all kinds of evil against you because of Me.*

*Rejoice and be glad, for your reward in heaven
is great; for in the same way they persecuted the
prophets who were before you.*
Matthew 5:10-12

I was good once I read them. I felt strengthened in my soul. What I
was experiencing was because of Jesus. He did not cause it; it happened because of my life with Him. And I was, and I am, willing
to endure persecution from anyone for Him. There was no way I
could turn back or back down from my faith in Him. Even though
Jesus had His eyes on me my entire life, I felt we were just getting
started because I was just getting to know Him.

Cherri and I have reconciled, and we have never spoken about
the incident. The revelation from God and His comfort brought
all the healing and the closure I needed. No need to rehash it. She
wouldn't remember the details anyway

That's not unusual. A person can yield to the demonic to such
a degree that they have no recollection of what was said or done
while under that influence. Evil spirits intentionally use people to
hurt other people.

We are to forgive the person, pray for their freedom, and take
authority over the spirit. Many people seek an apology before
they can forgive and move on. Scripture doesn't tell us to do that.
Apologies are nice, but they are not prerequisites for forgiveness.
Jesus said:

*For if you forgive others for their transgressions,
your heavenly Father will also forgive you. But if
you do not forgive others, then your Father will
not forgive your transgressions.*
Matthew 6:14-15 NASB

Forgiveness is an act of faith. When we choose to forgive, God
empowers us by His grace to do it. When I forgave by faith, my
emotions eventually lined up.

If someone in your life has hurt you, allow Holy Spirit to heal your soul. Release them. Say out loud, "Father, I forgive and release them."

Forgiveness is more for you than for the person you're forgiving. Unforgiveness can hinder your relationship with God and your ability to operate in His power.

Rats on the Roof

After college, I got an entry-level position at a marketing call center. Our responsibility was to answer questions from potential clients. I like talking to people, so I enjoyed working there. I was newly married, and the position allowed me to take care of my family.

The call center was extensive, with two shifts of workers. One shift started at 8:00 AM, and the other began at 5:00 PM. I worked during the morning shift. Most of the people who worked on the afternoon shift were students at a nearby Baptist Bible college.

During lunch, I would either talk to everyone in the break room or read. Everyone knew I was a believer. Some who were curious about God would ask me questions. Holy Spirit made them comfortable enough to ask, even though I had not been in Christ that long. Maturity and revelation come not from chronological time but from time spent with God.

Some of the younger women had secretly bet that they could get me to commit adultery, believing I'd waver in my commitment to Jesus and to Valerie. One woman dressed provocatively, staging "chance" encounters to get my attention. While that may not appear to be a form of spiritual warfare, it was.

One night, in a dream, the Lord revealed to me the spiritual dynamics of the company. In the dream, the LORD took me into the sky. Then we stopped abruptly, and I could see the marketing company. The roof of the building disappeared, revealing everything inside.

I saw what appeared to be rats running through the building in multiple directions—demonic spirits, the source of the temptress' actions, the evil agreement, and confusion

Holy Spirit gave me a strategy for dealing with it all. After following His strategy, I received a promotion providing tech support, an area in which I had zero knowledge. God blessed me to receive the training I needed—training that opened the door to a career in education.

I do not believe I would have received that promotion had I not listened to the LORD regarding the warfare, nor followed His supernatural strategy.

When it was time for me to leave that company, I left on a positive note, and the people showered me with love on my last day.

Avoid The Extremes

Spiritual warfare may manifest differently in different settings and different times. It's not always hours of binding and decreeing, nor is it something you can ignore, and hope it will go away. God may give you a single act of authority, then daily wisdom to walk out the win. I never used the strategies He'd gave me then again. I followed His instructions daily.

Wisdom is a spiritual weapon. Following the wisdom of God is one way of exercising the victory we have in Jesus over opposition. His wisdom enables us to arrest any spiritual activity in the atmosphere that is not of Him.

Some believers minimize the reality of spiritual warfare; others exaggerate it. Those who ignore it claim believers encounter warfare because they expect warfare; if their expectation is different, their experience will be different. I did not expect the warfare I experienced. I thought that once I accepted Jesus, He would teach me the truth about Himself, and I would follow Him, leading to a life filled with peace without challenges. That was not the reality.

Life is great with Jesus. However, those who desire to live godly will face challenges. I didn't expect demons to attack me, and I definitely couldn't ignore what happened. Satan had lost a false prophet and launched war against me.

However, we must be mindful not to go to the other extreme, believing that everything supernatural stems from the demonic realm, as if the demonic owns the supernatural. Some believe that everything supernatural that does not appear evil is of God, which is also not true.

To discern the difference, we must be sensitive to the voice of Holy Spirit and allow Him to reveal to us if what we are seeing or experiencing is from Him. This discernment from Holy Spirit is a necessity for the believer.

Take It By Force

From the moment John the Baptist declared, "Repent, for the Kingdom of Heaven is at hand," things shifted. It was the time of the fulfillment of prophecy when God's rule would be executed on the Earth in a way that it had not been since the fall of Adam.

> *From the days of John the Baptist until now, the*
> *kingdom of heaven suffers violence, and violent*
> *men take it by force. For all the prophets and the*
> *Law prophesied until John.*
> Matthew 11:12-23

Jesus experienced spiritual warfare from the time He was born of the virgin until He was crucified—from Herod's massacre of babies (Matthew 2), to the wilderness temptation, to constant confrontation by the religious leaders, to Judas' betrayal (John 13).

How did Jesus fight? Every miracle He performed was an act of spiritual warfare. Every demonstration of the Kingdom of God overthrew oppression.

Spiritual warfare is not always defensive. It is also offensive. We engage from an offensive position when we obey God, doing all He directs us to do.

CHAPTER 7

DISCERNING AND JUDGING SPIRITUAL EXPERIENCES

The Word, Not the WOW

Many people have spiritual experiences—some from God, some not. The challenge is discerning the source, especially if it does not appear to be "evil" or if a sense "peace" is felt. Our judgment cannot be rooted in the experience alone. We must not take the stance of "I saw it, so it must be true!"

We must learn to walk with God in a way that allows us to test our experiences against the Word. While everything Jesus said and did could not be written (John 21:25), everything He *is* saying and doing is based on what is written. That is why the Scripture admonishes us not to exceed what is written (1 Corinthians 4:6).

If a supernatural experience does not align with the Word, I've learned to ask God *how* it happened.

False Signs and Wonders

The supernatural is not a rare event that occurs beyond the natural. It is a dimension in which we operate as we come to understand the existence of the spiritual realm which constantly influences the natural realm. God, who has no beginning or end, created the spiritual realm. Since God created it and everything in it, supernatural experiences must be judged to determine their source— whether from God or a demonic spirit.

Signs, wonders, or perceived miracles cannot be our primary measure of judging. A sign may appear to be good or helpful to a person, but that doesn't mean it's from God. Demonic spirits will "help" in order to deceive people. Following signs alone can misalign us with God's plan for our lives.

Miracles, signs, and wonders from God are designed to point people to Jesus as Savior and Lord. False signs point to another spiritual entity, to created things—universe, planets, stars, an individual, self, or a level of "enlightenment."

Jesus warned that false Christs and false prophets would appear in the last days, performing false signs to deceive.

> *For false Christs and false prophets will arise and*
> *will show great signs and wonders, so as to mislead,*
> *if possible, even the elect.*
> Matthew 24:24

Note that Jesus said: "to mislead...*if possible*, even the elect." Some believers fear being deceived, and as a result, many misquote this passage, claiming that the elect will be deceived, but the Word says "*if possible.*" As a believer, you cannot be deceived if you continue to walk with Holy Spirit.

When we do not know the Word, we open ourselves to deception. We are prey, susceptible to accepting teachings that take Scripture out of context. Look at the deceptive signs that will occur when the person of the anti-Christ is operating in the Earth.

> *He performs great signs, so that he even makes*
> *fire come down out of heaven to the earth in the*
> *presence of men. And he deceives those who dwell*
> *on the earth because of the signs which it was given*
> *him to perform in the presence of the beast, telling*
> *those who dwell on the earth to make an image*
> *to the beast who had the wound of the sword and*
> *has come to life.*
> Revelation 13:13-14

The false prophet will perform signs, like making fire come down from the sky. People will follow this false prophet who points them to the anti-Christ because of the signs during this period of human history.

> ***And I saw coming out of the mouth of the dragon and out of the mouth of the beast and out of the mouth of the false prophet, three unclean spirits like frogs; for they are spirits of demons, performing signs, which go out to the kings of the whole world, to gather them together for the war of the great day of God, the Almighty.***
> **Revelation 16:13**

The source of these deceptive signs is demonic spirits. I want to highlight this to reveal this reality: demons will not wait until the Great Tribulation period to perform false signs. They are performing them today through false prophets for the sole purpose of deception. Every demonstration of power from demonic spirits is an attempt to imitate the power of God.

No spirit is equal to God. In the Book of Daniel, the magicians and diviners could not tell Nebuchadnezzar his dream, nor could they interpret it. Daniel was able to share the dream and the interpretation because God revealed it to him. This revelation did not come because of Daniel but because of Daniel's relationship with God (Daniel 2:19, 27-28).

In Egypt, Pharaoh's diviners imitated the signs God performed through Moses and Aaron. God strategically started with specific signs and then increased them beyond the diviners' ability. These spirits have limitations. God demonstrated that He alone is God to the Egyptians, the nations, those who worshiped spirits that presented themselves as "gods."

> ***Then the Lord said to Moses, "Say to Aaron, 'Stretch out your staff and strike the dust of the earth, that it may become gnats through all the land of Egypt.'" They did as God commanded.***
>
> ***The magicians tried with their secret arts to bring***

> *forth gnats, but they could not; so there were gnats*
> *on man and beast. Then the magicians said to*
> *Pharaoh, "This is the finger of God." But Pharaoh's*
> *heart was hardened, and he did not listen to them,*
> *as the Lord had said.*
> Exodus 8:16-19

The "gods" worshiped in Greek, Roman, and Egyptian "mythology" were spirits. They were demonic spirits that demanded specific sacrifices and rituals to be performed. We must be cautious about following the practices of our heritage or culture. It's OK to embrace your culture, but if you do, you must discern what constitutes a spiritual practice of worship and what does not. Many make the mistake of adopting a spiritual belief passed down by previous generations under the guise of cultural practice, then mix it with their faith. This is unholy mixing, and it simply does not work.

How Deception Enters: False Visions and Dreams

Deceiving spirits target the spiritually hungry, those burned out on religion, unlearned in Scripture, craving encounters. They prey upon those who desire more of God by presenting themselves as an answer to that heart cry. They appear as an angel of light (2 Corinthians 11:14), revealing some spiritual truth. They often attempt to discredit the Scripture, saying men have corrupted it, or by claiming to reveal some hidden truth, what the Bible calls "the doctrine of devils."

The experience is real, the interaction with a spirit is real. The message, however, is a lie. The peace or even love the person may feel is counterfeit, often just a pause in oppression. Yet, they believe they've had a divine encounter.

Spirits that "Taught"

Years ago, Thomas, a master-level medium in the organization, taught that George Hurley was the Holy Spirit in flesh. Thomas claimed that Adam had appeared to him and revealed some spiritual truths. Then Abraham appeared and did the same. When Abraham left, Jesus appeared, revealing spiritual truths. Lastly, George Hurley appeared with more truth.

Thomas claimed that each spirit taught him some deeper truth concerning the spiritual realm, reinforcing the teaching that each of these men was a Christ of a specific age in history.

Unfortunately, because Thomas believed in the teachings of George Hurley, he was open to this type of deceptive spiritual encounter. A counterfeit spirit took on the appearance of Jesus to deceive Thomas and cause him to teach spiritual principles from the demonic realm.

> *But even if we, or an angel from heaven, should*
> *preach to you a gospel contrary to what we have*
> *preached to you, he is to be accursed!*
> **Galatians 1:8**

Some believe if Thomas had known the Scripture, he could have discerned that this encounter was not from God. Unfortunately, he knew what the scriptures *said*, but didn't *know* the Scripture. To truly understand the Scripture, one must be able to rightly divide the Word. The organization used the Bible to support its teachings on spiritualism and mediumship.

Many inaccurate or incomplete teachings stem from an individual interpreting Scripture through the lens of their own perspective rather than what the Scripture actually says. We must not only know the Word but rightly divide it and receive revelation from God. Being able to quote a verse does not mean that the Word is in the person's heart. As we study and meditate on the Word, we will be open to the work of Holy Spirit, who reveals Jesus to us.

Tongues: Imitation or Real?

The Bible describes speaking in tongues as the ability, through the power of Holy Spirit, to speak supernaturally in either an earthly language that they did not study or a heavenly language. The organization taught that only master-level mediums could speak in a supernatural language, and not by their own will. A medium had to develop a level of sensitivity to yield to the spirit realm.

During one gathering, there was a moment when the expression of music and singing reached a high point. You could sense a strong spiritual presence. Congregants were "shouting" and running around the sanctuary. Suddenly, one of the master-level mediums yelled out and spoke in a supernatural language.

The beauty of having a relationship with God is that we can ask Him questions, and He will answer them because He wants us to know the truth. So I asked Jesus how it was possible for the medium to speak in tongues. Here is what He showed me.

The Bible says that tongues are a result of being filled with Holy Spirit, outward evidence of the inward filling.

> *And they were all filled with the Holy Spirit* and*
> *began to speak with other tongues, as the Spirit*
> *was giving them utterance.*
> **Acts 2:4**

I have identified two categories or types of tongues: the tongues of men and the tongues of angels. People will say there are more, but we must not confuse the type with how the supernatural language is utilized.

> *If I speak with the tongues of men and of angels,*
> *but do not have love, I have become a noisy gong*
> *or a clanging cymbal.*
> **1 Corinthians 13:1**

This verse reveals that one supernatural language is the language of men, and the other is that of angels. The languages of men are the languages spoken on Earth, including past and present languages. The tongues of angels are the languages spoken by the various types of angels. Demons are fallen angels; they have the language they used to speak in Heaven and learned the languages spoken on Earth.

When a medium yields to a demonic spirit, that spirit can speak through them. We often see this during demonic possession. That spirit may speak its former angelic language or an earthly language, whether it be a past or current language. When a demon causes someone to speak a language of the Earth, it may cause them to speak a language that is not typically spoken in an area or a language that is no longer spoken.

For example, if you are in an English-speaking country, the demon may speak French, Chinese, Arabic, or another language. The demon may speak English in an Arabic-speaking nation. It may even speak ancient Greek. This would give the impression of tongues as defined in Scripture.

We must exercise discernment when we hear someone speak in tongues to determine if it is from God or another spirit. Just because it is a spiritual language or a language that the people present do not know does not mean it is from God.

I'm sharing this so you will not be suspicious, but sensitive to God during those moments, allowing you to properly discern when something is of Him. Imitation tongues are a false sign. Genuine tongues are a sign from God and are full of power. We must distinguish between the real and the imitation. Supernatural demonstrations must not move us; we must be moved by God. The teaching, the sign, and the spirit behind the person must be tested.

Testing the Spirits

After my conversion, many master-level mediums, people I loved, approached me and said the "spirit" had given them the impression I was being led astray and was denying my true self. I immediately knew this was the working of seducing spirits, using people I loved, whose counsel I once received, to deceive me and get me to turn my back on Jesus.

Once, a relative in the organization asked me if I had tried the spirits. There was a lot of talk in the organization, just as there is in the Body of Christ, about trying or testing the spirits.

The Scripture does admonish us to test the spirits to see if they are of God. The problem is that many do not know how to test the spirits. They base the test on what they felt during an encounter. Spiritualists believe that any spirit that is loving, kind, and leads you to do good is a good spirit. Conversely, they believe spirits that attempt to harm you or someone else are evil. Spiritualists believe you can recognize a "good spirit" because you will sense love or peace when they come to you.

This belief does not accurately help a person test the spirits. Just because a person has an encounter and experiences peace doesn't necessarily mean it is the peace of God. Jesus told us in Scripture that the peace He leaves with us is not the same peace that the world gives (John 14:27).

There is the peace of God, and there's the peace of the world, which can be equated to peace that does not originate from God, and it is counterfeit. It is only absence, lessening, or pause from oppression. Many of the spirits I had once engage with, that I thought were kind and good, showed their true nature once I began walking with Jesus.

The feeling of love is no indicator that the encounter is of God. The demonic often tries to make people feel loved by hiding their true nature and intentions. They will speak kindly and politely to get a person to submit. Once submitted to, they have the legal right to fulfill their evil desires. There were two occasions when my mother allowed a spirit named Serapis to use her body. When asked why she did this, she said that she was familiar with this spirit, and it asked her nicely.

Many have had encounters and believe they were from the angel Gabriel. This has led to the start of religions founded upon the doctrine received from this spirit in disguise. Some have had encounters of Heaven and Hell. Some were from God; others were not. When we test those encounters against the Word and by the Spirit of God, we know which are counterfeit.

While we cannot debate someone's spiritual encounter, we can discern the source, judging the fruit, not the person. When this is not done, a person can get into error without realizing it. A person can be in opposition to God and think they are executing His will.

So, how do we test the spirits and the encounters?

Beloved, do not believe every spirit, but test the spirits to see whether they are from God, because many false prophets have gone out into the world. By this you know the Spirit of God: every spirit that confesses that Jesus Christ has come in the flesh is from God; and every spirit that does not confess Jesus is not from God; this is the spirit of the antichrist, of which you have heard that it is coming, and now it is already in the world.

You are from God, little children, and have over-come them; because greater is He who is in you than he who is in the world.
1 John 4:1-6

Verses two and three give us the key to testing the spirits: *every spirit that confesses Jesus Christ has come in the flesh is from God.* Deceptive spirits will say that Jesus is a Christ, an enlightened one, or a prophet who has reached the highest level of enlightenment. They will never admit that Jesus is God in the flesh, and He is Lord. Any spirit that appears as an angel of God will be able to say that Jesus Christ is God in the flesh and Lordy (1 John 4:2-3).

We read in verse 3 that every spirit that does not confess Jesus is not from God is the spirit of the Antichrist, which is already in the world. Many are waiting for the anti-Christ in flesh, but we must discern the spirit of the anti-Christ that is presently operating. Many "spiritual" teachings, such as manifestation, flow state, Theta healing, and yoga, just to name a few, are the result of teachings from the anti-Christ spirit.

Walk in Confidence, Not Suspicion

Receive this encouragement. You are from God; you have overcome the spirit of the anti-Christ, the false prophets in the world, and all deceptive spirits because greater is He, God, that is in you than he, the anti-Christ, that is in the world.

As you cultivate an intimate relationship with Jesus, you will not have to worry about being deceived. The Spirit of Truth lives in you, is with you, and is upon you. You are also in Him. He will lead you into all truth; you cannot be deceived.

Unfortunately, those who are open to deception are those who do not know God. If you would like to learn in greater detail how to judge spiritual experiences, discern false signs and false teachings, and experience authentic encounters with Jesus, join my mentorship community. Go to jamalmaxsam.org/cu.

CHAPTER 8

PERVERSION OF THE GIFTS: RESTORING

GOD'S INTENT

Spiritualism often perverts the gifts of God—altering them from their intended purpose to a distorted or corrupt use. Many are taught, just as I was, that there is a difference between spiritualism, often referred to as white magic, and black magic. There isn't.

The only difference between "white" and "black" magic is the intent and the level of deception. Those who practice black magic do so with the intention of harming others; they know who they serve. Those who practice white magic believe they are doing good, not realizing they are actually causing harm. The spirits that respond to incantations from "white" and "black" magic are the same. They are demons.

All Gifts Are from God

Every spiritual gift comes from God and was placed in us before we were born.

> *Every good gift and every perfect gift is from above, and cometh down from the Father of lights, with whom is no variableness, neither shadow of turning.*
> **James 1:17 KJV**

Some of those gifts will only function when we are connected to God; others will function by will.

Satan cannot give gifts. All he can do is deceive a person into misusing their gifts that God has given. Many mediums, psychics, witches operate in a perversion of the prophetic gift—trained to be sensitive to the spirit realm, but not to the Spirit of God. Familiar spirits will then speak to them and through them, producing counterfeit "signs." That, in part, is how George Hurley was able to amass such a large following—false signs and wonders.

How Psychic Readings Really Work

When a person receives a reading, the message or "insight" comes from a familiar spirit, not from God. The medium may claim to be a clairvoyant (a seer), clairaudient (a hearer), or clairsentient (a hearer). When they "feel" something related to the emotional state of others, they may refer to themselves as an empath.

Unfortunately, the term "empath" has become popular, especially in business circles. The word originates from the Greek word *"empatheia,"* meaning passion or affection (ChatGPT). Psychologists use it to describe the ability to understand and share the feelings of others. Spiritualists see it as the ability to sense and experience the emotions and energy of others.

Believers should never identify themselves as an empath. While the word itself is not demonic, its use places believers in a category they need not be in, since the ability to sense the emotions of others is part of the gift of discernment and word of knowledge in some people.

In my training, I was taught to say, "When I come into your vibrations…" indicating I had stepped into the person's energy and could sense what they were releasing.

A medium cannot know a person's past or present, nor can they perceive a person's emotions. They sense the thoughts and impressions projected by a familiar spirit. If the person receiving the reading accepts those thoughts, they become seed sown in the soul, impacting emotions, behavior, and speech.

Other tools of divination are tarot cards that are interpreted based on the meaning of the cards and the order in which they were turned over. Then there is what I call the "yes-or-no" reading. A medium asks the spirit a question while holding a necklace, and the familiar spirit causes the necklace to swing one way for "yes" and another for "no."

God Works Through Our Five Senses

Demonic spirits imitate the way God communicates. God speaks to a person, and they may perceive, sense, or experience something through one or more of the five senses. God designed our five senses to interact with Him. There is no "sixth sense." That is a term used to describe something beyond the natural.

Jesus is our example; He used all His senses when He engaged in the supernatural. As a believer, you and I do the same. All our senses are designed to function multi-dimensionally, equipped to engage in the natural and supernatural realms. We must yield our members as instruments of righteousness (Romans 6:13).

Inside the Altar: The System that Groomed Us

Every location in the organization had an altar. The altar staff, all virgins dressed in white robes, tended it. We lit the candles and the incense, rinsed the altar seven times before placing the oil and water on it. We also recited prayers as the attendees brought silver coins, placed them in trays, and anointed their foreheads. They'd then make the sign of the cross and receive from the spirit of George Hurley.

I served because I truly wanted to serve God, and I took the responsibility seriously. Eventually, I left the altar staff to train for mediumship, believing that was the next step toward "enlightenment." Honestly, I was ready to date; I didn't want to be held to a vow. The organization emphasized the importance of self-control and purity.

The purity was more ritualistic, aimed at making us conduits for the spirits. I had to take spiritual baths to cleanse my spirit, soul, and body. These baths included special oils, patting myself dry with my hands so the cleansing was not contaminated.

In Christ, purity is not a ritual, but the result of the inner work of Jesus. His blood cleanses us and makes us pure. Bathing in oil and slapping ourselves dry doesn't rid us of spiritual contaminants. It's the blood of Jesus! We steward that purity by carefully watching what we allow into our souls.

Holiness, or purity, is a state of being; it is a spiritual position we attain by faith. It's not a dress code or a regimen. A religious perspective of holiness has led people to strive for something in their own strength that they can only receive by faith. The religious form of holiness that focuses on externals fosters bondage and a judgmental spirit.

Jesus wants you free, and so do I.

Protect the Children

The enemy targets children early, sowing seeds of the occult that shape their lives—unless Jesus frees them. Satan's desire is to pervert the purposes and gifts that God has placed in children. The Scripture highlights the vulnerability and the necessity of helping children cultivate an intimate relationship with Jesus.

> *Train up a child in the way he should go, even when*
> *he is old, he will not depart from it.*
> **Proverbs 22:6**

When the Word is planted in a child's spirit and soul, when they grow and mature, that which was planted will produce fruit. The primary influencers in a child's life are their parents. We must teach them the Word, intimacy with Holy Spirit, and how to use their gifts to fulfill their God-ordained purposes and destiny.

With the proper direction, our children can come to understand that hearing the voice of Holy Spirit is the norm. Visions and dreams, and engaging with Him in the supernatural will not be something out of the ordinary. If parents do not teach them these things, they are open to demonic influence because of their susceptibility and curiosity about spiritual things.

When I served as a youth pastor, many children shared their dreams and visions from God with me. By God's grace, I helped them understand what to do with those visions and dreams. When I worked in the public school system, children shared that they had "evil dreams" and had seen the devil. I know it was Holy Spirit that allowed the children to feel comfortable enough to share those experiences with me.

I heard a testimony of a woman who saw dark shadows, spoke to them out of curiosity, and was slowly discipled into witchcraft—first by spirits, then by online sources. She began reading the Satanic bible, and eventually joined a coven. But praise God, He delivered her from witchcraft! Curiosity without teaching and guidance becomes a doorway into the occult.

If we equip our children, they can avoid what happened to that woman. As we help them understand the supernatural of God, they will know the truth; there will be no place for demonic deception. They will recognize the counterfeit, partner with Holy Spirit, and exercise their authority in the name of Jesus to make demons flee. They will learn how to engage with God's angels, unafraid, what to do with dreams and visions, how to speak prophetically, lay hands on the sick, and watch them recover.

We can teach our children to do what Jesus did and release the power of God to bring freedom to their friends and classmates.

CHAPTER 9

MEDIUMSHIP CLASS AND FALSE PROPHETIC TRAINING

After leaving the altar staff, I began attending a mediumship class at the Hagar's School of Mediumship and Psychology. It was the next logical step to learning deeper spiritual truths and how to use my gifts (or so I thought).

Hagar's School of Mediumship and Psychology

The classes in Hagar's School of Mediumship and Psychology, taught by master-level mediums, were designed for students to learn how to give psychic readings, work with specific spirits, and deepen their meditation practice to interact with the spiritual realm to a greater degree. Classes were held once a week, and students were required to fast before class and wear all white.

Each student received a wand used for meditation, healings, and readings. A Hebrew word was etched on it, and we were told the spirit would reveal its meaning as we meditated. We also studied the significance of oils, incense, and candle colors—what to burn for "warfare," what to use to attract love, money, opportunities, or intensified experiences. We were taught to build personal altars and were required face east at designated times to meditate.

Incense: Biblical vs. Unbiblical

Exodus 30 describes the altar of incense and the incense God specified to be burned on it as worship to Him. This incense was used exclusively to worship the LORD, foreshadowing Christ and His "once-for-all" sacrifice, and mirroring heavenly realities (Revelation 5:8; Acts 10:4).

Spiritualists often quote passages from Exodus to justify the use of altars, oils, candles, crystals, stones, and incense to communicate with spirits. They have been deceived into believing their practices are of God. They are not! God did not designed us to encounter Him that way. Using these items opens doors to the demonic. Just because something is "spiritual" doesn't make it godly.

As believers, our lives are an expression of worship to God! Every act of worship—every prayer, every act of love and kindness—ascends before Him like incense. He honors it.

> *When He had taken the book, the four living creatures and the twenty-four elders fell down before the Lamb, each one holding a harp and golden bowls full of incense, which are the prayers of the saints.*
> Revelation 5:8

> *And fixing his gaze on him and being much alarmed, he said, "What is it, Lord?" And he said to him, "Your prayers and alms have ascended as a memorial before God.*
> Acts 10:4

The condition of our hearts and the source of motivation determine if the fragrance is sweet-smelling or foul. As we submit to the process of transformation, spend time in His Presence and walk in obedience to His Word, we become that perfume that pleases Him.

Manifestation and the Law of Attraction

In our mediumship classes, we were trained to "manifest" or attract what we wanted. We see this in the Law of Attraction, a form of spiritualism that encourages individuals to attract what they desire rather than posturing themselves to receive what God desires for them. Believers do not need to "attract" anything; we are already blessed, every need met in Christ.

One problem with "manifestation" is self-will. Though it sounds biblical because it borrows language from Scripture, it removes the need to submit to God. Divination and witchcraft are rooted in self-will. God knows what is best for us and has made it available to us as we submit to His will. Lack of submission to God is a culturally polite way of saying rebellion.

> *"For rebellion is as the sin of divination, And insubordination is as iniquity and idolatry. Because you have rejected the word of the Lord, He has also rejected you from being king."*
> 1 Samuel 15:23

Today, manifestation practices, especially as taught in many business and self-help circles, are a perversion of the principles of faith. By faith, we receive (take ownership) of that which God has already given it to us. We must believe we have received it, then we will see it in the natural.

Many believers have criticized this teaching, and as a result, live and operate in a place beneath God's intention for them. Satan, then, uses this deception to lead them into the practice of manifestation.

People may see results through "manifestation"—desired opportunities, money, or even a spouse—but at what cost? Satan does not mind us having "success" as long as we don't have an intimate relationship with Jesus. We were created for intimacy with God. These techniques only move us away from Him.

Unfortunately, many believers engage in manifestation practices, believing them to be innocent. There are only two sources from which we receive: the domain of darkness or the Kingdom of God. Nothing from the domain of darkness can be considered harmless.

Before attempting to "attract" something to you, ask, "Is this God's will for me? Is this His best for me?" Some things God is OK with you having or doing, but that may not be His best for you. Trust that God has already made it available, and exercise your faith to receive it. Remember, you can't "10-step formula" God.

> *...seeing that His divine power has granted to us everything pertaining to life and godliness, through*

*the true knowledge of Him who called us by His
own glory and excellence.*
2 Peter 1:3

*Delight yourself in the Lord; And He will give you
the desires of your heart.*
Psalm 37:4

Biblical Meditation vs. Spiritualist Meditation

Let's take a moment to understand Biblical meditation to avoid unholy mixing, which happens when teachings that are not of God are mixed with His principles.

What is meditation? There are two Hebrew words used in the Old Testament that are translated as meditate. The first is found in Genesis 24:63. Isaac went into the field to *meditate* in the evening. The Hebrew word for meditate here is *suwach* (Strong's #7742), meaning to muse pensively, contemplate, study, meditate.

The next time we see meditate used is in Joshua 1:8. God instructs Joshua to meditate on the Word day and night and not to allow the Book of the Law to depart from his mouth. The Hebrew word here is *hagah* (Strong's #1897), which means to murmur, implying pondering, imagining, and meditating. *Hagah* also means to roar, speak, or study.

Biblical meditation is studying and pondering the Word of God, and it differs significantly from that practiced by spiritualists and others. I was taught to mediate by clearing my mind, which is like opening the door to your house and allowing anything and everything to enter. Biblical meditation helps us to know Him and hear what He is speaking to us as we fill our minds with God's Word.

Today, unbiblical meditation is believed to have health benefits and is used for relaxation and self-care. But, as we've pointed out before, just because something appears harmless and beneficial in many ways, it does not mean it is Scriptural.

The deception of unbiblical meditation is the sense of peace or calm a person feels when they practice it. When they begin to experience confusion or frustration again, they return to meditation to find a place of peace and calm once more.

I reiterate that this type of meditation opens a door to demonic spirits. When the participant feels a sense of peace, it is not the peace of God; it is simply an ease of torment. Once this door is open, demonic spirits may not attack immediately, leaving the person ignorant to what has happened.

These spirits are predatory. They may often attack in another area or even lie dormant for a period, waiting for the opportune time to strike.

If you want to clear your mind, find relief from frustration, or seek help with a behavior, use the Word of God. Discover what it says about any issue or problem you're dealing with. Declare that Word over yourself.

Spend time in the Presence of God through various types of prayer.

Knights of the All-Seeing Eye

Soon after I began mediumship class, I joined the Knights of the All-Seeing Eye, a secret society within the organization modeled after the Masons. The Masons, a secret society and fraternal order for men, originated as a professional organization for architects. Unfortunately, their focus shifted to use spiritualist teachings as a form of personal growth and development.

We were taught about the "third eye," located in the center of the forehead. Anointing a person in that spot awakened the spiritual eye. This belief aligns with the concept of chakras from Eastern religions. It is unholy mixing, and is pure deception!

The initiation ritual of the Knights of the All-Seeing Eye occurred at night. We were blindfolded and led around in circles amid strange sounds, then made to kneel on what felt like rocks.

"What do you want the most at this moment?" one of the facilitators asked.

"I want to be a good knight," replied one of my fellow initiates.

Another repeated, "I want to be a good knight!"

"Stay down there, then," a facilitator said, laughing.

They wanted a specific response, and I was going to figure it out.

I wasn't concerned about being a "good knight." My knees hurt, and I wanted to stand up.

The facilitators came to me. "What do you want most?" they asked.

"To get up," I said.

"Stand up." Everyone after me answered the same way.

Each aspect of the initiation had a spiritual and symbolic meaning, but I didn't fully understand what they meant. By the grace of Jesus, I was not around long enough to learn.

God does not require us to participate in any initiation ritual to go deeper in Him. You do not have to be part of a secret society to learn the mysteries of God; He reveals His mysteries freely to us by Holy Spirit (1 Corinthians 2: 7-10).

Fasting

In the organization, everyone fasted on Fridays until 6:00 PM. As a member of the Knights of the All-Seeing Eye, I fasted on Mondays and Wednesdays until mediumship class ended. Fasting was an essential discipline, intended to cultivate spiritual discipline and increase sensitivity to the spiritual realm, which it did. It did heighten my sensitivity, but it also created a distaste for fasting.

After Jesus set me free, I only fasted when our pastor called a corporate fast—typically once per year. Holy Spirit never pushed me to fast nor allowed me to feel condemned when others talked about their encounters during and after a fast. I never felt like I was missing out on something. I would rejoice with them while enjoying my chicken sandwich (until I stopped eating chicken).

Over time, Holy Spirit reframed fasting for me. Now, when He invites me to fast, I do—as He directs me. Not only does it increase our sensitivity to Holy Spirit, but according to Scripture, it is also one way that we minister unto the LORD.

Fasting does not move the hand of God, nor does it cause breakthrough or the supernatural to happen. Fasting moves us. It enables us to be in greater alignment with what God is doing, saying, and has already done through the finished work of the cross.

I have heard many believers say that they were fasting for a breakthrough. I understand what they mean and the intent of their hearts. God is inviting us to realize that breakthrough occurs in and through our lives because of our covenant relationship with Him through Jesus.

We don't work for breakthrough; we align with breakthrough. We should not approach fasting as if it were part of a formula that causes things to happen. When we do, we might miss what God wants us to receive during the fast. We should recognize that fasting is a means to increase our sensitivity to God, assisting us to experience all that He desires during that time, and the months and years that follow.

> *While they were ministering to the Lord and fasting, the Holy Spirit said, "Set apart for Me Barnabas and Saul for the work to which I have called them." Then, when they had fasted and prayed and laid their hands on them, they sent them away.*
> Acts 13:2-3

The Difference Between A Medium and a Prophet

Many spiritualists claim that mediums are prophets. Most mediums do have a prophetic gift because the gifts and callings of God are without repentance. Although a medium or psychic may have a prophetic gifting, they are not prophets. They are not using the gift for God's purposes. The Scripture is very clear about mediums and spiritists, and God's disapproval of those practices. This was a hard lesson for me to learn because I had been taught that the words "prophet" and "medium" were interchangeable.

If a person had explained the difference to me then, I most likely would have rejected it and been in denial. But you can't reject or deny when Holy Spirit shows you something plainly written in the Word. It is undeniable and irrefutable. I was heartbroken to know that the gift God had given me had been used for demonic purposes. All I could do was weep, repent, then rejoice in the reality that, by God's grace, I had the opportunity to be His prophet as I was born to be.

A medium is one who learns how the spirit world operates

to communicate with and manipulate spirits. This differs from psychics, who receive messages from spirits. Those who engage in witchcraft focus on incantations, using objects and words that cause spirits to make things happen.

The goal of a medium is to manipulate spirits to achieve specific outcomes in the natural realm. The first mention of the word "medium" is in Leviticus 19:31.

> *Give no regard to mediums and familiar spirits;*
> *do not seek after them, to be defiled by them: I am*
> *the Lord your God.*
> **Leviticus 19:31 NKJV**

The phrase "familiar spirits" comes from the Hebrew word *owb* (Strong's #178), primarily connected with the occult practice of consulting the dead, means "a conjured spirit, a medium, or a leather bottle." It refers to a conjurer who professes to call up the dead through magic, especially to give revelation about future uncertainties. They call on the spirits of family members, friends, spiritual mentors, others they respect, or ancestors.

Many celebrities confess to having consulted a psychic or medium. Some even claim to be mediums or psychics themselves, believing it to be a gift. They are seeking answers beyond the natural means, which we all do. *How* we seek those answers and where we go in search of them is vitally important.

Believers seek God; and we position ourselves to give godly solutions to those who do not know Jesus as Savior and Lord. God is gracious and merciful, but very serious about preventing demonic spirits from leading people astray.

> *"When you enter the land which the Lord your*
> *God gives you, you shall not learn to imitate the*
> *detestable things of those nations. There shall not*
> *be found among you anyone who makes his son or*
> *his daughter pass through the fire, one who uses*
> *divination, one who practices witchcraft, or one*
> *who interprets omens, or a sorcerer, or one who*

casts a spell, or a medium, or a spiritist, or one who calls up the dead. For whoever does these things is detestable to the Lord; and because of these detestable things, the Lord your God will drive them out before you. You shall be blameless before the Lord your God.
Deuteronomy 18:9-13

When Holy Spirit took me to these verses, I stared at them for a long time as the reality of what I'd been doing sank in.

These Scriptures should not be used to judge or condemn, but to guide and reveal God's intention for those using these spiritual practices. Satan uses a variety of methods to deceive and mislead people into employing dark arts, even though they may call themselves light workers.

While there is much more that I could say about this, I primarily want to highlight the structure that was put in place to pervert the gifts within a person. Everyone is born with spiritual gifts that enable them to fulfill their God-given purposes and destiny. Spiritualism desensitizes a follower's ears to the voice of God and develops those gifts for demonic purposes.

Freedom in Christ enables us to hear His voice and use our gifts for His glory.

CHAPTER 10

PROPHETIC PEOPLE, HOLY SPIRIT POWER, AND KINGDOM MATURITY

I believe that so many people are attracted to mediums and psychics because far too many people have never encountered a believer who operates prophetically. And yet, God has given *every* believer the ability to hear His voice and speak what they hear. He has placed prophets in the Body to equip and train His people to operate prophetically (Ephesians 4:11-13).

God calls us to greater spiritual maturity to demonstrate His power by His means.

That All May Prophesy

In the Old Testament, we see the school of the prophets. Though we don't read about them in the New Covenant, that doesn't mean they no longer exist. They exist in a different way.

Under the New Covenant, Holy Spirit is poured out on every believer, giving us all the ability to operate prophetically. This is the fulfillment of what was written in Joel 2:28-29.

> *And it shall be in the last days,' God says,*
> *'That I will pour out My Spirit on all mankind;*
> *And your sons and your daughters will prophesy,*
> *And your young men will see visions,*
> *And your old men will have dreams;*
> *And even on My male and female servants*
> *I will pour out My Spirit in those days,*
> *And they will prophesy.*
> Acts 2:17-18

Every Spirit-filled believer can operate in the prophetic, though not all are prophets. God's plan is that wherever His people are, His voice is released. Far too many believers don't realize that they possess this ability, or they have not developed it. Some believe they must have the gift of prophecy or be a prophet to operate in the prophetic. This belief hinders God's people from operating as they have been designed.

It is important to distinguish between the ability to operate in the prophetic and the gift of prophecy. Some believers have been given the gift of prophecy, which allows them to operate in higher dimensions of the prophetic.

> *Since we have gifts that differ according to the grace given to us, each of us is to exercise them accordingly: if prophecy, according to the proportion of his faith;*
> **Romans 12:6**

Training is the Role of the Worship Fellowship

The Church is designed to be a place where believers develop in the prophetic. Without active training in the worship fellowships, people may be drawn to the occult by seducing spirits that take advantage of the person's hunger to experience God more deeply.

Jesus gave people as gifts to equip the Body of Christ to use what He has deposited in it.

> *And He gave some as apostles, and some as prophets, and some as evangelists, and some as pastors and teachers, for the equipping of the saints for the work of service, to the building up of the body of Christ; until we all attain to the unity of the faith, and of the knowledge of the Son of God, to a mature man, to the measure of the stature which belongs to the fullness of Christ.*
> **Ephesians 4:11-13**

Every believer is prophetic. Training enables us to impact the lives of others and advance the Kingdom of God.

Influence in Every Sphere

Prophets are an essential gift in maturing believers and equipping them to fulfill their purposes and destiny. For believers to accomplish all God has for them, they need to know how to operate in the prophetic. Prophetic people receive the counsel of God on behalf of others; they speak the solution that people desperately need. The use of the prophetic is not to be limited to worship gatherings.

If the prophetic is confined, those who do not know God may consult a medium. The prophetic can be used in every circumstance and environment. We must not think prophesying is about speaking in King James English, or saying, "Thus says the Spirit of God." You can speak what Holy Spirit tells you to speak in plain language, then allow Him to do the rest.

When believers do not exercise their gifts in the different areas of cultural influence, we leave the culture exposed to demonic spirits. Johnny Enlow, the author of *The Seven Mountain Prophecy,* identified these areas as: religion, education, government, business, entertainment, media, and family.

Occult organizations dispatch mediums, witches, and wizards in every area of influence in a ploy to control those areas. If the enemy can influence these areas, then he can exercise control over the Earth, which has been given to believers. If we are not the influencers in a territory or sphere of influence, then they are submitting to whoever is operating as the influencer.

Imitators, Not Originators

When believers operate in the prophetic and use their gifts in their assigned areas of influence, they will quickly see how occult demonstrations are not equal to the power of God. The magicians of Egypt imitated every supernatural sign that God used Moses and Aaron to perform...up to a point.

When God turned the dust of the ground into gnats, the magicians in Egypt could not do the same, and told Pharaoh it was "the finger of God" (Exodus 8:16-19). Jesus told the religious leaders of the day, that if He cast out demons by the "finger of God," then the Kingdom of God had come upon them. The operation of the gifts God has placed within you is one of the ways people see God's power at work and the demonstration of the Kingdom.

Growing in the Prophetic

To mature in your gift, you must allow yourself to be mentored, discipled. So many believers have scattered, isolated themselves, and disconnected from the local worship fellowship for various reasons, primarily hurt from imperfect leaders. Isolated believers may operate from zeal and may have knowledge, but often lack wisdom, which prevents them from winning souls. Proverbs 11:30 tells us, "he who wins souls is wise." If the enemy can separate a believer from community and development in their gifting, their effectiveness is minimized.

We must be grounded in the Word if we are to mature in our gifts. The spirit of prophecy is the testimony of Jesus (Revelation 19:10), and Jesus is the Word made flesh. All spiritual gifts identified in Scripture operate through faith in Jesus. Faith comes by the Word (Romans 10:17).

So faith comes from hearing, and hearing by the word of Christ.

Word, Power, and Balance

It is possible to have a high degree of revelation and understanding in the Word, but not in the use of spiritual gifts. It is also possible to function in the gifts with a great degree of accuracy without much knowledge of the Word. We need both.

Teaching without demonstration reduces the Kingdom to a philosophy, perspective, and mental assent. Worship gatherings become concerts that include motivational speeches that move the soul, but have little or no Kingdom impact. Demonstration of power without the Word leaves people in a state of immaturity, running from encounter to encounter, and basing their relationship with God solely on demonstration of His power.

Immaturity causes believers—even highly gifted ones— to falter when life challenges them, and they have to stand on the Word. Because they operate at a high level in their gifts, they may believe they are somewhere in their faith and relationship with God that they are not. This is the breeding ground for error. We must allow God to mature us as He places us in positions of influence.

In Power and Demonstration

The Kingdom of God is not merely in words, but in power (1 Corinthians 4:20). Faith serves as the catalyst for the demonstration of signs, wonders, miracles, and divine intervention.

There is a difference between signs, wonders, miracles, and divine intervention. Miracles, signs, and wonders are supernatural demonstrations by Holy Spirit to draw people to Jesus as their Savior and Lord. All of them defy natural laws, natural ability, and anything else that can be accomplished with human strength and ingenuity; it points to the sovereignty and power of God.

The focus of these demonstrations should always point people to Jesus. Some miracles are what I call sovereign miracles. A sovereign miracle, sign, or wonder occurs when God demonstrates His power without the believer's involvement. For example, a person is healed without anyone praying for or laying hands on them.

Then there are what I call "collaborative miracles," which are miracles that are performed through the believer. Someone being healed when a believer lays hands on them is a collaborative miracle.

Divine intervention, on the other hand, is when the supernatural happens on behalf of the believer. God enforces His covenant with the believer, manifesting their covenant rights and benefits.

Workers of Miracle

I believe that believers are not called to pray for, fast for, or believe for miracles for themselves. While I believe God honors those who do, I also believe God has extended an invitation to walk with Him in a deeper way—to be instruments of the miraculous. We cannot be consumed with trying to receive miracles for ourselves if we are to be the vessels through which they happen for others. We must enter a new realm of faith and power where we are confident that God will make things happen supernaturally for us. He will handle all that concerns us because we are in covenant relationship with Him through Jesus. As a result of this covenant, God will demonstrate His power, however needed, to bring His plans for our lives to pass. That's exactly what He did in delivering the children of Israel from the bondage of Egypt, and by sending an angel to rescue Peter from prison (Acts 12:5-17).

When examining the life of Jesus in Scripture, I see Him working miracles, not receiving them. He said that we would do the same works He did and even greater works because He went to the Father (John 14:12).

The key is knowing this reality: once Jesus ascended and went to the Father, Holy Spirit entered the Earth and came upon and dwells within every believer. It is Holy Spirit who performs the miraculous through us and continues to perform signs, wonders, and miracles greater than those Jesus performed while physically on Earth. This is not blasphemy; it is walking in the reality of what Jesus spoke about every believer in the Scripture.

CHAPTER 11

GIFTS ON PAUSE

With all I had seen and done in the domain of darkness, you might assume that once I gave my life to Christ, I just flowed prophetically. Not so. Even after God told me I was His prophet, there was a season where it seemed as if God had pressed the pause button on my gifts, allowing me time to become solid in my understanding of the Word. He was ensuring I would stay free of deception and unholy mixing. The supernatural without the Word leads to deception; the Word without power roots us in religion.

The Pharisees are a prime example. They knew the Scriptures well, and yet accused Jesus of blasphemy when He declared Himself God's Son (John 10:33). They accused Him of casting out demons by a demonic ruler (Matthew 12:24). They witnessed in Jesus a level of authority they did not possess, and they mislabeled it. They could not or would not discern the truth.

The demonic realm has marketed fear and associated anything supernatural with their power —an intentional ploy to cause believers to shy away from the supernatural. As a result, many believers operate more from superstition, ready to rebuke everything, than from the supernatural of God.

Training in the Quiet

While attending Word of Life, my prophetic gift was dormant. I studied, learned, served, and developed spiritual discipline—personally and within the community of believers. After some time, I began using my musical gift, playing alongside Tom, a powerful worship leader. Through him, God introduced me to prophetic worship and playing in the Spirit.

At times, during the musical expression, God would tell me,

"Stop playing, and just listen." I didn't fully understand why, but I knew I had to obey. God may give us illogical instructions that will produce supernatural results without telling us why. We must simply obey, knowing our obedience pleases Him and fulfills His will.

I now know that during those times, God was imparting something to me through Tom. Tom never prophesied with words, but prophesied on his keyboard. After singing the planned songs, we would move into an open, free prophetic flow. At times I could sense the flow, but Holy Spirit restrained me from playing— *Just listen.* On a few occasions, God allowed me to join in, but most of my prophetic expression took place in private.

This impartation lasted for years. When the time came for Tom to no longer serve as the lead musician, he laid hands on me, and I stepped into that role. By God's grace and my submission to His process, the worship expression at Word of Life never missed a beat. I stepped right into the stream Holy Spirit had established, and He expanded it through me.

I still didn't prophesy through words. I could sense when a prophetic word was about to be released, and played prophetically as it came forth. I could hear the voice of God, but was not released to speak.

I began to think my prophetic expression was limited to teaching and playing. But what I thought was discernment was really a self-imposed limitation, rooted in my negative perspective and disguised as "discernment."

Focused on One Gift, Limiting the Others

During that season, I focused on another area of my calling—pastoring. I spoke with my pastor, and he began developing me in that area. I taught pre-service classes, helped lead prayer as part of the prayer team, taught at both Sunday and Wednesday gatherings, and later, pastored the youth.

I want to note that youth ministry was not, and should never be considered a "stepping stone." I was not working my way up. Promotion in the Kingdom of God is not like corporate ladder-climbing; it's obedience. Every step of my journey allowed me to grow as I exercised my gifts. My heart has always been to serve God and His people. I trusted that God would bring to pass everything He'd said concerning my purpose and destiny. I never tried to position myself with people. That often leads to bondage.

Promotion comes from God. When you set your heart on Him and obey Him, He will bring the right people in your life. We can think we are ready to operate in a particular role, such as pastor, prophet, business owner, but not be fully prepared. Only God knows the weight that comes with positions or assignments. He prepares us to carry that weight. We must submit to the process and allow Him to mature us. When we do, God will fulfill His promises to us, not only to blessing us, but blessing others through us.

Not for the House Alone

Many believers limit the operation of their gifts to the worship fellowship, the local church. They begin to pressure the pastor to allow them to speak or to ordain them because they are called to the "ministry." But everywhere God sends us is a place of "ministry." Our gifts were never meant to be confined to one setting.

> *But to each one is given the manifestation of the*
> *Spirit for the common good.*
> 1 Corinthians 12:7

Many may not know what that looks like in the context of their careers. Every believer is called to use their gifts to draw people to Jesus. Not every believer is called to do that within the four walls of a worship fellowship. As we consider Ephesians 4:11-16, some are called specifically to equip the Body of Christ—within a worship fellowship or in different contexts.

A Move, a Mentor, a Breaking Open

My perspective about my prophetic gifts and calling shifted when God moved us to Cincinnati, Ohio. Valerie and I were both working in a school. Val desired to move from the classroom to school leadership, and I wanted a full-time teaching position, having earned my teaching license. An opportunity opened up in Cincinnati. But

I refused to chase career opportunities; I was in pursuit of God's Presence, and I had to know He was in the move.

Holy Spirit confirmed that He was sending us to Cincinnati in multiple ways. I didn't realize there was a divine connection await-ing me to equip me to further walk out my purpose and destiny. Several years earlier, I'd briefly met Apostle John W. Stevenson, a pastor, anointed musician, songwriter, and worship leader. He had traveled to Detroit for a worship conference and would be rehearsing at Word of Life. My pastor had asked me to unlock the building and turn on the sound equipment for him.

"Hello, I'm John," Apostle Stevenson said.

I introduced myself, and he went to the keyboard and began playing a song he'd composed, "Jehovah Reigns." Once the worship team members arrived, I left. I did not see or speak to him after that.

Ten years later, on my first day in a new school, I was walking down the hallway and I heard one of my co-workers singing.

"*Jehovah reigns forever! Jehovah reigns forever! Jehovah reigns forevermore!*" he sang joyfully.

"I know that song!" I exclaimed. "John W. Stevenson wrote it."

"He's my pastor!" my co-worker blurted.

After a brief exchange, he invited me to HEIRS Covenant Church. When I visited HEIRS, I experienced God's presence in a way I'd never experienced before. His presence was so weighty, and I cried through the entire gathering. Apostle John's message was "The Convergence of Synchronized Destinies." I immediately knew that God had sent me to Cincinnati to align me for the next phase of my destiny by connecting with a community of like-minded believers.

Still, I took my time. We visited other fellowships—including those connected to Word of Faith and those founded by graduates from Rhema Bible College. I wanted solid teaching of the Word and the power and presence of God, not just emotionalism and excitement.

And while there was nothing wrong with the places we visited, I recognized that Holy Spirit had a specific place for Val and me.

Peace to be Planted

I continued tithing to Word of Life until God planted us where He wanted us in Cincinnati; it was important that I honored God with my tithe and seed. I also stayed connected with the pastor.

As I shared with him my search for a fellowship, he said one thing that settled me: "Jamal, it's not about finding a church like Word of Life; it's about finding the place God wants you to be."

I felt peace, and, after our third visit, Val and I made HEIRS Covenant Church our home.

We can, at times, step into the new season, expecting it to be like the old season. Humans are comfortable with the familiar. However, new spaces are just that —*new*. The constant between the old and the new is Jesus. We must look for Him as He leads us into new seasons in our lives and be willing to embrace them.

I recognized that Apostle John was not only *an* apostle to the Body of Christ, but he was (and is) *my* Apostle. I immediately saw our shared DNA; we are both songwriters, musicians, producers, authors. He is a prolific teacher and prophet, with a powerful revelation on the Kingdom of God, solidly rooted in the Word of God. And he is intentional in stewarding God's Presence. In that environment, under his leadership, God broke my self-imposed limitations. My gifts were no longer on pause.

At HEIRS, I developed and grew in the prophetic. The "pause" had done its work; I was rooted and grounded in the Word of God, more disciplined, and prepared to carry the greater weight of the call. The environment, leadership, and assignment were now unlocked.

Right Place; Right People, Right Time

Some aspects of your life are location and people-specific. Specific individuals have been assigned to help you grow and develop in your gifting, and to help you birth your God-given purposes and destiny.

Some limitations can only be broken in specific atmospheres. Some things with the LORD are taught, while other things are caught. You must be in an environment where the supernatural power of God is demonstrated, taught, and activated.

We are living in a time in the Body of Christ when every believer must have their gifts activated. The operation of your gifts is essential to the fulfillment of your God-given assignments, purposes and destiny. You must allow God to plant you in the right place, with the right voices so you can flourish. Your gift(s) respond to revelation and faith. When you are planted in the right soil, hearing the right voices, there are no limits to how God can use you!

A Prayer and a Charge

My prayer for you is that you do not allow any limitations—self-imposed or placed on you by others— to hinder the expression of that which God has place in you. I pray that scales are removed from your eyes, and you recognize the treasure in you.

I pray that you understand all the great things the LORD purposes to do through you to demonstrate the reality of His Kingdom. Some people will not believe until they see (Exodus 7:9). God wants them to see demonstrations of signs, wonders, and miracles through you so they may see and believe on Him. He has equipped you for that very reason.

Father, in the Name of Jesus, remove every self-imposed limitation. May the person reading this book be planted in the right place, with the right leaders, for the right assignment. Let Your Word anchor them and Your Spirit empower them. May every dormant gift be activated, so that through them, others see Your Kingdom come on Earth as it is in Heaven. Amen!

CHAPTER 12

JUST KINGDOM

Many reject "organized religion," specifically Christianity, for many reasons. Some reject it after seeing hypocrisy or having been hurt by other believers, especially those in leadership. Others reject it because Scripture may have been used out of context to justify certain behaviors and lifestyles, or even to manipulate.

My heart breaks that so many now claim to be "spiritual, not religious." They believe in the existence of God and seek spiritual experiences apart from "religion." Unfortunately, they seek those experiences apart from Scripture as well. That is the deception and danger of being "spiritual."

I posted this statement on social media: "I am not spiritual. I am not religious. I am Kingdom!" Someone called it hate speech. We live in a time when everyone can express and affirm their beliefs loudly to the world—everyone, it seems, but believers in Christ. When we share who we are in alignment with God's Word, we are often misunderstood, even denigrated.

Teaching about the Kingdom of God is not as common as it should be, nor is it as readily understood. Some have not heard about the Kingdom, or think Kingdom is a radical concept. We must have a clear revelation about what it means to be "Kingdom."

What Spiritualism Is…and Isn't

When someone says they are "spiritual," they are affirming that they believe in the reality of spiritual beings and the spiritual world. Spiritualists understand that humans are spirit beings with a soul that lives in a body, and when the earthly experience ends, life continues in the spiritual realm. They also believe that once a spirit enters the spiritual realm, it can assist others in navigating the natural realm.

Many spiritualists believe that every "kind" spirit is of God, from God, and is part of God, declaring the we are "God within." Many who engage in spiritualism will look within themselves for to the spirit or guidance. They seek to have spiritual experiences that will enhance their lives, cause success, enable them to help others, and reach a higher level of enlightenment.

When a person seeks guidance from their own spirit, they may be led by whatever has been deposited in their spirit, placing their faith in the source of the deposit—whether God, human, or demonic. Submitting to that guidance, gives the spirit permission to be their lord.

Believers look only to Holy Spirit to lead us into all truth. We seek God alone for encounters with Him. He is our Creator; our spirit comes from Him. When we accept Jesus as Savior and Lord, God becomes our Father, and His Spirit comes to live within us not because our spirits are a part of Him, but because Holy Spirit has chosen to live in us. Our spirits are distinct from Him, and we commune with Him through our spirit.

Those who channel spirits often teach that any spirit claiming to be the only way should be ignored and not trusted. However, Jesus said He is the *only* way.

> **Jesus said to him, "I am the way, and the truth, and the life; no one comes to the Father but through Me.**
> **John 14:6 NASB**

Spiritualism focuses on enlightenment, believing that the different levels of the spiritual realm represent levels of enlightenment that a person can experience as they learn and master certain spiritual principles and character qualities. Spiritualism claims to acknowledge Jesus, but it views Jesus as a master teacher, prophet, or a Christ, not *the* Christ. He is placed on equal footing with Buddha, Muhammad, Abraham, Moses, and other spiritual teachers, whose teachings build upon those of others, and all play a role in revealing the "truth" to humanity.

Heaven and Hell

Even though spiritualism teaches about the reality of the spiritual world, it denies the existence of Heaven, Hell, and the reality of the work of the Cross. They teach that Heaven is a state of the mind that impacts outward life, and Hell is a deplorable condition of the mind and spirit that impacts physical life. With the denial of Heaven and Hell, comes the denial of the work of the cross and its necessity for the redemption of humanity.

Those of us who believe in Jesus Christ believe that the crucifixion was necessary to save humanity from sin and restore right relationship with God. That relationship prevents us from experiencing Hell, which was not made for people, but for Satan and his demons. God sends no one there. Unfortunately, some unknowingly choose to go there by rejecting God's love expressed through Jesus.

The Word of God

Spiritualists take Biblical principles and revelations about God out of context and apply them to their doctrine of the spiritual world. Some truth mixed with deception makes the deception more believable.

They teach that the Bible has been tampered with, altered by people to manipulate and conceal the truth, a belief that is popular in Islam. Since the Bible has been "tampered with,'" only someone "spiritual" can interpret its symbolism, see past the alterations, and to extrapolate hidden truths.

Spiritualists believe that every spiritual teaching and religion presents a different perspective of "the truth." All religions are branches of one tree, with various ways of serving the same "god." The Bible, the Quran, Hindu teachings, Buddhist teachings, and the writings of other spiritual teachers all lead to truth.

Religion Within Christianity

While many beliefs today are classified as a "religion," I want to focus on religion (adhering to laws and doctrine) and its impact within Christianity. Religion outside of Christianity represents souls who need to know Jesus as Savior and Lord. Religion *within* Christianity is a spirit that brings bondage, hurt, falsehood, and turns people away from Jesus rather than drawing them into a closer relationship with Him.

Religion focuses on the appearance of godliness but denies its power. It makes adherence to rules, the law, the measure of righteousness, and substitutes academic analysis of the Scripture for revelation from Holy Spirit. Knowledge without revelation opens the door for religion. Scripture tell us this would be the case in the last days.

> *... holding to a form of godliness, although they have denied its power; Avoid such men as these.*
> 2 Timothy 3:5

Religion appears authentic, but this verse highlights that an authentic relationship with God results in His active power at work.

Religion focuses on rule-keeping, and causes people to work to earn what God has freely given. It often equates salvation with attire, facial hair, and other regulations designed by man. The focus is on avoiding punishment and following a formula to achieve results.

Religion can cause a person to *attend* church instead of *being* the Church. Church attendance may be more about the emotional high of the experience or fulfilling a weekly obligation. Religion often causes people to be judgmental rather than judging fruit (Matthew 7:1-5, 20 7:20).

Religion is critical and prideful, based on the letter of the law, not the spirit. It makes us unable to hear what God is saying, focusing only on what He has said. A religious person will quickly denounce anything beyond their paradigm, thinking it couldn't be God. They do not take the time to ask God if something is of Him. Religion reduces God to formulas.

Years ago, I wrote and produced R&B and rap music for various artists. After giving my life to Christ, God spoke to me about writing, recording, and producing music for believers.

I acted immediately. I held auditions for singers for a group we called Perfect Praise. We traveled around the Metro Detroit area performing original music. After some time, I realized that performing with the group Perfect Praise was not how God wanted *me* to do music.

Holy Spirit revealed that the vehicle was gospel rap music. I began writing, producing, and performing rap music that glorified Jesus. I started rapping at Word of Life and traveled the area, hosting and participating in concerts for youth and young adults. Every concert included encouragement to live for Jesus, with an invitation to receive Him as Savior and Lord. Many teenagers gave their lives to Christ and received prayer for any issues or concerns in their lives. God moved powerfully.

I was part of a movement of God, using rap music to win a generation of souls. Everyone could see this was God, right? Wrong. I reached out to various churches, asking about the possibility of doing a concert for their youth ministries.

"Gospel rap was not of God," one pastor said.

My response was similar to Peter's when questioned about ministering to Gentiles at Cornelius' house. I explained all God had done through gospel rap. The pastor and many others stood firm: *Gospel rap was not of God.* I believe those pastors were so blinded by how rap music had been used for ungodly purposes that they could not see how God could use it to win souls. They failed to discern the fruit that could come from it.

Religion will cause people to miss a move of God. A person trapped in religion can discern demons, but not always discern God. They may label something demonic when God is restoring its original, holy purpose to use it for His glory.

Two Extremes

There are two extremes into which the demonic pushes people to prevent them from experiencing all God has for them. On one end of the spectrum is religion which classifies anything supernatural as demonic. On the other end is spiritualism, which believes that everything of a spiritual essence that does not appear evil is of God.

Some who are dissatisfied with religion and have a desire for more, are often pushed toward spiritualism. This begins subtly through unholy mixing, then gradually moves the person to be entirely out of alignment with God.

97

Spiritualism may cause a person to miss spending eternity with God. A religious person who has accepted Jesus as their Savior will spend eternity with God, but they may miss fulfilling all God intended them to accomplish in the Earth. They will have little impact on Earth.

The Kingdom Perspective

God intends for His people to live with a revelation of His Kingdom. When we do, we understand the difference between principles, spiritual laws, and religious rules. We understand the distinction between a spiritual discipline and a rule imposed by religion, which may have little or no spiritual impact.

We, first, must understand what the Kingdom is. The explanation in this book provides a short overview of the Kingdom. I encourage you to study the Scriptures and allow Holy Spirit to speak, giving you the Kingdom perspective.

The Kingdom is God's eternal rule that encompasses all creation, whether visible or invisible, known or unknown. In the Scriptures, Jesus, when teaching, often said, "The Kingdom of Heaven is like…" He spoke of the Kingdom of God during His time on Earth, and He continues to speak to His people now.

> *From that time, Jesus began to preach and say,*
> *"Repent, for the kingdom of heaven is at hand."*
> *Jesus was going throughout all Galilee, teaching in*
> *their synagogues and proclaiming the gospel of the*
> *kingdom, and healing every kind of disease and*
> *every kind of sickness among the people.*
> Matthew 4:17,23

The Kingdom was also a central part of John's message, as he baptized people to prepare the way for Jesus (Matthew 3:1-3). When Jesus sent out the twelve, He instructed them to perform signs and wonders, and declare that the Kingdom of God had come (Matthew 10:5-8).

As the Body of Christ, we have somehow strayed from the message of the Kingdom, focusing on specific aspects of it. Salvation is vital; it is how we become citizens of the Kingdom and children of God. Jesus told Nicodemus that no one can see the Kingdom unless they are first born again (John 3:3). Thus, there is the necessity for winning souls. After the soul is won, they must learn how to operate in the Kingdom, which is why Jesus instructed us to make disciples.

> *"Go therefore and make disciples of all the nations, baptizing them in the name of the Father and the Son and the Holy Spirit, teaching them to observe all that I commanded you; and lo, I am with you always, even to the end of the age."*
> Matthew 28:19-20

Salvation is about more than ensuring the souls of people escape Hell; it is about restoring them to God's original intent— living as those created in His image and fulfilling the commission He gave Adam (Genesis 1:26-28). When we receive Jesus as LORD and Savior, we also receive His Kingdom.

> *Wherefore we receiving a kingdom which cannot be moved, let us have grace, whereby we may serve God acceptably with reverence and godly fear:*
> Hebrews 12:28-29 KJV

> *For He rescued us from the domain of darkness, and transferred us to the kingdom of His beloved Son...*
> Colossians 1:13

Many in the Body of Christ have used the words "Kingdom" and "church" interchangeably, but they do not have the same meaning. The word "church" in Scripture, as used by Jesus, refers to the *Ecclesia.*

The Greek word *"ekklesia"* means "called out," referring to a governing body. God calls us out of darkness, places us into His Kingdom, and makes us a part of His ruling, governing body—the Church. Believers are to *be* the Church, not just attend church. We gather at worship fellowships where we find community and are equipped to fulfill our purposes and destiny. In the worship fellowships, we learn how to operate as the *Ecclesia* on earth, the benefits of our covenant with God, and how to be heirs of God and joint-heirs with Jesus.

Understanding that we *are* the Church helps us to embrace the Kingdom perspective. Apostle John W. Stevenson defines the Kingdom perspective as:

> **The Kingdom Perspective is a constant awareness of Jesus, who is King, and His Kingdom, which encompasses all things. It is an awareness of the spirit realm that is in operation and the spiritual authority we have in it through Jesus Christ. It is the acknowledgment that Jesus has all power and authority in Heaven and in the Earth, and as His ambassadors, we have been given that power and authority to influence, impact, and affect the natural and spiritual realms for the advancement and the establishment of His Kingdom throughout the Earth!**

When believers operate from a Kingdom perspective, they realize that the gifts, talents, and abilities God has given them are to be used in various areas of cultural influence. They stop limiting the demonstration of God's power to a worship gathering. When we adopt the Kingdom perspective, we recognize that "ministry" is everywhere God sends us.

You are not on your job until God releases you for ministry. Your current employment is your ministry; you are there on assignment. That assignment is specific to you and involves demonstrating the Kingdom. You did not start your business solely for financial reasons. God led you to start it because it is an instrument that reveals the Kingdom of God.

Believers with the Kingdom perspective are unstoppable. As the Body of Christ re-embraces revelation of the Kingdom of God, we position ourselves to demonstrate signs, wonders, and miracles. These signs will greatly surpass the limited demonstrations of demonic power. I will discuss this more in a later chapter when I discuss operating in miracles in your assignment.

Then God said, "Behold, I am going to make a covenant. Before all your people, I will perform miracles which have not been produced in all the earth nor among any of the nations; and all the people among whom you live will see the working of the Lord, for it is a fearful thing that I am going to perform with you.
Exodus 34:10 NASB

CHAPTER 13

AVOID UNHOLY MIXING

As we operate in the Kingdom, we must discern and avoid unholy mixing. Unholy mixing occurs when teachings, doctrines, and principles sourced from the demonic realm are blended with the principles of God; it is mixing the unholy with the holy. Unholy mixing is often disguised as spiritual practices that do not appear to be evil and can frequently produce seemingly positive results.

God is holy, and His children, created in His image, are called to live from that holy identity. Everything we do must flow from the place of holiness. When anything unholy is added, the result is compromise.

The eighth chapter of Ezekiel gives a clear picture of unholy mixing. It identifies the people of God—leaders in this context—engaging in practices with other spirits behind closed doors. This unholy mixing hinders the expression of God's presence.

> *And He said to me, "Son of man, do you see what they are doing, the great abominations which the house of Israel are committing here, so that I would be far from My sanctuary? But yet you will see still greater abominations."*
>
> *So I entered and looked, and behold, every form of creeping things and beasts and detestable things, with all the idols of the house of Israel, were carved on the wall all around. Standing in front of them were seventy elders of the house of Israel, with Jaazaniah the son of Shaphan standing among them, each man with his censer in his hand and*

the fragrance of the cloud of incense rising. Then He said to me, "Son of man, do you see what the elders of the house of Israel are committing in the dark, each man in the room of his carved images? For they say, 'The Lord does not see us; the Lord has forsaken the land."
Ezekiel 8:6,10-12

Everything appears to be as it should on the surface, but we can sense something is off.

Ezekiel 8 also highlights women engaging in a ritual of weeping for Tammuz, a spirit worshiped as an idol. Then God shows Ezekiel men with their backs to the temple facing east, prostrating themselves eastward toward the sun, a spiritualist practice (Ezekiel 8:16).

Unholy mixing is not a new phenomenon. We see it throughout the Scripture, and, as we have already seen, as far back as the late 19th century, the spiritualist movement spoke of the Aquarian Age, multiple Christs, and repeated "prophe-lies." Jesus warned us of this:

For there shall arise false Christs, and false prophets, and shall shew great signs and wonders; insomuch that, if it were possible, they shall deceive the very elect.
Matthew 24:24 KJV

Some labeled this mixture as "Christianity," misinterpreting Scripture to justify the use of mediumship and occult practices as a result. Sadly, today, some people identify as Christian but have not accepted Jesus as their Savior and Lord. Just because something is labeled "Christian" does not mean that it is truly Christian.

Jesus also spoke to this in Matthew 7:22-23:

On that day many will say what they did in His name and the Father would respond, "I never knew you, depart from Me, you who practice lawlessness."
Matthew 7:22-23

Some people possibly love Jesus, but teach things that are not of God because of unholy mixing. They have been deceived, and teach that deception to others. For more teachings, check the "Dismantling Spiritualism" series at Champion University.

Avoiding Unholy Mixture

I am convinced that in these times, discernment is a necessity, not a luxury, for every believer. Many believe discerning of spirits refers only to discerning the demonic. But we need to discern God. We need to discern the times, as well as how God is moving, so we can be aligned with Him (1 Chronicles 12:32). Discernment enables us to see what is happening in the spiritual realm as we operate in our authority as believers.

Believers must also be able to discern the devices of darkness, but not out of fear. We have already overcome the demonic. Still, we cannot allow ourselves to be ignorant of Satan's devices (2 Corinthians 2:11).

Unholy mixture often slips in because it appears harmless on the surface. Often, demonic agendas are hidden behind music and entertainment. It becomes mainstream and culturally acceptable. Many dismiss it, thinking it is "not that serious." We must remain sensitive to Holy Spirit, listening for His voice regarding every detail of our lives, including what we listen to, what we watch, where we go, and even the social groups we join.

Unholy mixing happens when we lose the reverence of God for the sake of inclusivity and cultural relevance. We must not compromise, allowing sin into the house of God in the name of love. There is a difference between loving people, not judging them, and condoning their beliefs. We must love all people while not condoning beliefs or lifestyle choices contrary to Scripture.

Furthermore, unholy mixing occurs when people seek to experience God and the supernatural apart from the Word and Spirit of God. I hope you see throughout this book the dangers of unholy mixing. It starts small, then, before we know it, we are far away from the truth of God.

You were running well; who hindered you from

obeying the truth? This persuasion did not come from Him who calls you. A little leaven leavens the whole lump of dough.
Galatians 5:7-9

We are to be the light in dark places. Being the light does not mean being religious or tense. It also does not mean being carnal to fit in. It does not mean compromising. Paul spoke of becoming all things to all men so he could win some (1 Corinthians 9:22). We must learn to meet people where they are, without compromise, and boldly love them to Christ.

CHAPTER 14

WINNING A SPIRITUALIST: WHAT DIDN'T WORK

The divine timing of God that day in Detroit is undeniable. It was one week before graduation from Hagar's School of Mediumship and Psychology. Jesus interrupted my life, and saved me from making a covenant—a binding agreement— with repercussions I didn't fully understand. Many around me thought I'd lost my way. But I had actually found it.

It took the audible voice of God to arrest me. Others had tried evangelistic methods on me that failed. So let's discuss a few of those methods to see why.

Street Witnessing

"If you died today, do you know where you would go?" some well-meaning believer, a total stranger, would ask me. They'd, then, hand me a brochure about Hell, Heaven, and the need for salvation through Jesus. The approach seemed more like a door-to-door or car sales technique—share the features of Heaven, talk about the agony of Hell, and ask, "Where would you rather be?"

It didn't work for several reasons. First, I had no level of relationship with the person. Why would I believe what they were saying? Secondly, there was no demonstration of the power of God. They were kind and friendly, but I didn't sense the presence of God. I'm not saying Holy Spirit was not with them. I just did not experience Him through them.

Besides that, I didn't believe in Heaven and Hell, but they didn't ask me what I believed. I saw their idea of salvation as being rooted in their misinterpretation and misunderstanding of the Bible.

Those who witnessed to me did nothing to help me see.

As far as I knew, I was serving Jesus. When I told them I believed in Him as a Christ, they seemed confused. They neither said nor did anything to help me see He was *the* Christ. They'd leave, offering to pray for me, or, if I frustrated them enough, they'd snap, "God bless you!" and walk away.

Unfortunately, that method of evangelism doesn't introduce people to a relationship with Jesus. It often causes those people who do come to Him to do so out of fear, not love.

If you are going to witness to or evangelize someone you do not know, demonstrate the power of God when you do it. This is why the prophetic, signs, wonders, and miracles are needed. Develop your gifts so you can give a word of wisdom, a word of knowledge, heal, or demonstrate His love in some way that draws them to Him. You may reveal what the person is experiencing or has experienced in the past, along with the thoughts and intent of their hearts (1 Corinthians 14:24-25, Hebrews 4:12).

Seeing His power, makes it indisputable that God sent you to them. At that point, they must decide how to respond to God's invitation.

Confront and Expose

One tendency of believers when dealing with someone in the occult, new age, or spiritualism is to confront and expose them. The negative impact of some reality television programs has fueled a desire to publicly expose wrongdoing and shame individuals who do wrong. God will give wisdom on when and how to expose something.

It is one thing to speak against a particular teaching or doctrine; it is another to speak against the person. We must use caution when speaking against a person. Know for a certainty that is what God is asking you to do. Follow as He directs, in love and with wisdom.

We see in the Scripture that Elijah confronted the prophets of Baal publicly (1 Kings 18:20-40); it was necessary for Israel to turn away from serving Baal. John the Baptist addressed the Pharisees; Jesus turned over the moneychangers' tables. These examples might lead one to believe that this is the method to use every time.

There is a time for confrontation (and I would add prophetic confrontation). As believers, we cannot allow our zeal for God or our dislike for what we see to be the determining factor. God must determine the time and method of exposure that He will use to He draw people to Him.

There is a grace on my life to dismantle; it is one of the phrases God uses when He refers to my assignment. I've participated in the confront-and-expose approach. I've learned to dismantle the teaching and restore the person who was trapped in its bondage. God desires for false teachers and those who follow them to be saved. I know what it is like to believe a lie and call it truth.

A friend of mine once shared a story of how he debated a Muslim and won the debate. He said that he was so excited that he shared the experience with another friend. The friend asked one question that changed him forever (and had a profound impact on me): *"You won the debate, but did you win the soul?"*

We must understand that it's not about debating to prove ourselves "right." God is after the individual's soul. Debates can bring offense, and an offended person is more challenging to win than a fortified city (Proverbs 18:19). I emphasize the importance of using wisdom—the wise win souls.

> *The fruit of the righteous is a tree of life, And he*
> *who is wise wins souls.*
> **Proverbs 11:30 NASB**

A Painful Example…And a Do-over

My mother had started a spiritualist church in Sarnia, Ontario, Canada, and due to a conflict in schedule, she asked me and my cousin, Cherri, to lead a service.

We agreed and went to Sarnia to facilitate the service.

There were about 15 people in attendance that day. After teaching, I asked, "Does anyone have any questions?"

A young blond woman, accompanied by her father, stood, and read a passage from 1 Samuel 28 that warned against consulting mediums.

"Mediumship and communicating with familiar spirits are not of God!" she said firmly.

I was familiar with the passage and immediately responded. But to my dismay, my response was one commonly used to justify this unbiblical practice. It was based on a misinterpretation of the passage.

"The issue," I said, "was not that King Saul consulted a medium or spoke to Samuel's spirit, but that God had rejected Saul. God wasn't responding to Saul's prayers through the usual means because of the rejection. So Saul used the medium to communicate with Samuel through a familiar spirit."

I focused on Samuel's response, which was, "Why are you disturbing me when God has rejected you?"

"The rejection made it wrong, not talking to Samuel's spirit," I said confidently and with conviction. All the other deceived agreed and marveled at my "wisdom."

My confidence shut the young woman down. She didn't know how to respond; she sat quietly through the rest of the service.

I deeply regret how I misused and misinterpreted God's Word and shut down one of His daughters. She came out of concern and probably had warned her father about spiritualism. She most likely prayed for her father's freedom from deception. And when the opportunity arose, she courageously spoke up for the LORD. If only she'd known more of the Word to rebut what I'd said. If only she had spoken of other instances proving mediumship was wrong, saying my explanation was taken out of context, and that I did not consider the entire Scripture.

People of God, my prayer is that you allow Holy Spirit to give you what to say in the moment, and that you speak His Word with authority, power, and wisdom. I pray that you will allow God to give you wisdom, insight, and revelation into His Word so you may share with accuracy all that He is revealing to you.

CHAPTER 15

WINNING THE SPIRITUALIST: WHAT WORKED

After giving my life to Jesus as my LORD and Savior, Holy Spirit began to show me the people He used to draw me to Him, even when I was unaware. Just as He revealed the events that unfolded that day in Detroit, He also showed me moments throughout my life when His hand was guiding me—through conversations, prayers and relationships that I didn't recognize at the time.

We must remember that no one can accept Jesus as LORD and Savior except by Holy Spirit.

> *Therefore, I make known to you that no one speaking by the Spirit of God says, "Jesus is accursed"; and no one can say, "Jesus is Lord," except by the Holy Spirit.*
> 1 Corinthians 12:3

God draws people to Jesus, but He uses us to partner with Him. We may plant; we may water; God gives the increase (1 Corinthians 3:6). Remember, winning souls is not a sales process; it's not done through persuasion or pressure. We don't have to seal the deal. We just need to be sensitive to how God will have us to interact with the individual as He does the work within their heart.

> *"No one can come to Me unless the Father who sent Me draws him; and I will raise him up on the last day. "It is written in the prophets, 'And they shall*

all be taught of God.' Everyone who has heard and
learned from the Father, comes to Me.
John 6:44-45

Each person who crossed my path had a part in the process. They didn't argue or force; they lived their faith before me and prayed faithfully for me

Questioning the False

When I was fifteen or sixteen, I began dating Danielle, a singer and pianist, from a kind, faith-filled family. I was writing music and performing as well, and we met through a television program, where I frequently performed.

Many of the other performers frequented the show, and we naturally formed friendships. I did not know Danielle, but she knew who I was, and told the other performers that we were dating. Danielle had "blocked" me.

After hearing the rumor, I figured I should at least meet the person I was supposedly dating. So had I our mutual friend set up a "surprise" meeting.

Danielle and I connected right away. She and her family were believers, attending a Baptist Church down the street from the spiritualist church I attended. I visited her church on a few occasions, mainly to support her and the choir—not because I wanted to learn about Jesus. I rarely paid attention to the messages.

One day, we sat on my patio, talking. She told me about a dark season in her life. She'd experienced trauma, and feeling hopeless, she cried out to God. "If You're real, please come and help me!"

And He responded; Jesus came to her.

Then she asked me, "If what you believe is true, why didn't George Hurley come to you?" The same question that God would later ask me.

I tried to answer, fumbling for an explanation.

"Maybe Jesus had to come to you because of your level of spiritual maturity."

Danielle wasn't having it. "When I was at my lowest point and cried out to God, why did I encounter Jesus and not George Hurley?"

I had no answer. I sat quietly, angry because I did not know how to respond.

"I want you to think about what you believe," she said.

We sat in silence for few a minutes as I processed the question. Then she changed the subject.

That question became a seed that Holy Spirit and those He sent my way would water until I gave my life to Christ.

Danielle's parents became aware of my spiritualist beliefs through a book my mother had published. They distanced themselves from my mother, but never from me. They continued to love on me. After I gave my life to Christ, I saw Danielle once more and thanked her for the part she played. And although I never got a chance to thank her parents, I've always been grateful for their love and kindness.

The Power of Prayer

Not long after my relationship with Danielle ended, I got a job working at a fast-food restaurant. Although I had a lawn care business that generated a decent profit, I took the job to be with my friends. That decision turned out to be another divine appointment.

One of the managers, Colleen, led the afternoon shift that I often worked. She was kind, steady, professional. Between serving customers, I would frequently discuss various topics with the other employees. I'd share my spiritualist beliefs with anyone who was open to hearing them.

One day, Colleen interrupted the conversation, and I could tell she was frustrated. She did what typical fast-food managers do when the employees are not working; she redirected me to work. She never spoke to me about Jesus. She never debated or challenged me about my beliefs. She demonstrated kindness and love toward me while ensuring I didn't have time to share my beliefs with others.

A little over a year after coming to Jesus, Holy Spirit gave me a vision of Colleen praying for me. I hadn't known she was a believer, but she had prayed for me daily to come to know Jesus and to be delivered from deception. I was overcome with gratitude and wanted to express my thanks to her.

"I want you to know that I accepted Jesus as my Savior and Lord," I told her sometime later.

"Yes! Thank God!" she shouted with so much joy, a huge smile on her face.

Colleen told me she'd overheard my conversation that day, and her spirit was troubled. "Holy Spirit, I don't know what he is into, but it isn't right."

She cried out to God for my salvation from that day on.

Overwhelmed, I thanked her again, grateful to God that He divinely positioned her to hear those conversations so she'd intercede on my behalf. I thought I was there to be around my friends; God placed me there to be covered with prayer.

A Living Example

Sometime later, I met Jineen, a cashier at the grocery store near my grandmother's house. She was a few years older than I, which I did not mind. I spent time with her, hoping to date her.

One day, I asked her if we could spend some time together, perhaps watching a movie at her apartment. She agreed. I prepared for that first date—haircut, cologne, carefully chosen outfit.

"What movie are we going to watch?" I asked when I arrived.

Jineen grabbed the remote and turned on the TV. Not to a movie, but Christian TV. I spent my first date watching Creflo Dollar, Joel Osteen, and other preachers.

But I wasn't deterred.

As we spent more time together, talking and enjoying one another's company, watching Christian television and listening to the Word became the norm.

One day, Jineen and I were discussing our perspectives on money. She told me that she followed the Biblical principles of tithing and giving.

"When I was unemployed, I couldn't give or tithe as I desired," she explained. "So now that I have a job, I'm saving a portion of my wages to give the tithes I was unable to give."

She did it, not because she had to, but because she wanted to out of her love for God.

That impacted me.

Eventually, our schedules shifted, and we saw each other less frequently, until we lost touch.

After giving my life to Jesus, He showed me that conversation. He had used Jineen's love for Him to draw me, and I wanted to thank her.

One day, while working at the fast-food restaurant, I heard a familiar voice at the drive-thru. I walked over to the window just as Jineen drove up. I smiled!

"I want you to know that I am a believer now. I accepted Jesus as my Savior and Lord," I said gratefully. "I want to thank you for how you live your life before God; it really impacted me and helped me come to Jesus."

I shared in greater detail how watching her relationship with God prepared my heart to encounter Him. Then I encouraged her to keep walking intimately with Him. Tears filled her eyes as she thanked me.

God used her love for Him to awaken love for Him in me.

The Common Thread

Each of these people—Danielle, her family, Colleen, and Jineen—played a role in my salvation. None of them argued theology with me. None of them compromised their convictions. They used truth, love, prayer, and lifestyle to point me to Christ.

Because of them, I am now walking in purpose and destiny, and God is using me to impact the lives of many. All that He does through me is a direct result of those who prayed for me, planted seeds or watered them. Every life I touch, every soul I rescue from deception, every life I point to Christ is part of their eternal reward.

Love, prayer, truth spoken without judgment, faith lived without compromise! That is how we win the spiritualist.

Chapter 16

How to Handle a Spiritualist Family Member

If you have a friend, family member, coworker involved in spiritualism, the occult, or New Age, your response to them must be Spirit-led. While every believer is called to make disciples, we must be clear on our role in each person's life. God may provide a different approach for each person you meet who engages in spiritualism. For some, He may tell you to distance yourself because they are not your assignment. For others, He may assign you to pray for, as Colleen did for me. With some, God may have you talk with periodically to plant or water. He may tell you to invite some to your worship fellowship. And God may use you to demonstrate His power through prophecy, a miracle, a sign, or a wonder with some.

The key is discernment to know how Holy Spirit leads without allowing our desires or frustration with the occult to lead us.

First, Pray

If you have a family member trapped in the occult, my advice is to first pray for them. Pray that the blinders be removed from them, break the spirit of deception, and ask Holy Spirit to send a Holy Spirit-filled believer to speak His Word in a way they can receive it.

If you have received the baptism of Holy Spirit, you should pray in your supernatural language. Praying in tongues is the highest form of prayer; we are praying beyond our understanding, praying from our spirit, and yielding to Holy Spirit as He intercedes.

In the same way, the Spirit also helps our weakness;
for we do not know how to pray as we should, but

*the Spirit Himself intercedes for us with groanings
too deep for words.*

*And He who searches the hearts knows what the
mind of the Spirit is, because He intercedes for the
saints according to the will of God.*
Romans 8:26-27

*For if I pray in a tongue, my spirit prays, but my
mind is unfruitful...*
1 Corinthians 14:14

Be open to occasions when Holy Spirit may orchestrate an opportunity for you to share with them.

Take Authority, Walk in Wisdom

When your family member comes to your home, you have the authority to prevent any spirits they entertain from entering your house.

Make a declaration stating that your family member or friend can enter your house, but every spirit that is not of God cannot set foot on your property in Jesus' name. Pray this prayer to prevent some spirits from entering with them. An invitation to your family member is not an invitation to the spirits they entertain.

This is not superstition, nor is it a license to operate in fear or zeal without wisdom. These are spiritual laws that evil spirits try to use to their advantage. We must know how the spiritual realm works.

God said that His people perish because of a lack of knowledge (Hosea 4:6). Understand this: when you engage with someone, you are not only engaging with them, but also with the spirits they engage with. When people interact with you as a believer, they have the opportunity to experience God through your relationship and covenant with Him.

When you visit your relative's home, they are in authority. While you operate in a superior authority because of the covenant with God through Jesus, you cannot cast demon spirits out of someone else's house without their consent. However, you can arrest them and prevent them from operating while you are there.

You do this by decree. Declare, in Jesus' name, that every spirit that is not of God must cease its activity while you are visiting. Where you go, the presence of God and His Kingdom go. This decree will allow you to spend time with your family without dealing with any challenges in the realm of the spirit.

If you have a friend who engages in the occult, allow Holy Spirit to reveal to you how you are to respond. Many of the strategies I've shared apply to friends as well as family. You should pray for them using the prayer suggestions mentioned earlier.

Remember: you have authority and power over all the power of the enemy, and nothing can hurt you (Luke 10:19). Do not allow fear or superstition to cause you to think any powers of darkness can or ever will stop you.

When They Come Out

When a person comes out of new age, occult, spiritualism, witchcraft, Satanism, they will need support, patience, and understanding. Living in the domain of darkness can be a traumatic experience. The degree to which they were involved determines the degree of trauma that occurred and the soul healing that is needed.

I know some who were delivered from voodoo and had experiences where demons raped them. Others experienced attacks like I did. Some experienced worse attacks, where the demonic spirits tried to orchestrate accidents that could have resulted in physical death. Many have experienced attacks similar those mentioned earlier in this book.

Some believers call it backlash. "Backlash" occurs when Satan retaliates against a believer for thwarting his plans. Some believe a person only experiences backlash because they expect to. Neither perspective is wrong. It is not cut and dry. I didn't anticipate the backlash I experienced. I thought after the encounter with Jesus that "every day would be sweeter than the day before." It wasn't like that for me. I didn't expect demons to manifest in dreams, then continue the attack once I'd awakened. But it happened, and it didn't stop until I had a revelation of my authority in Jesus and used it.

You have authority in Jesus. You don't need to pray, asking God to do something that He has already done by giving you the authority to address. I referred to this verse earlier, but I want you to read it in several different translations and get it in your spirit.

Behold, I give unto you power to tread on serpents and scorpions, and over all the power of the enemy: and nothing shall by any means hurt you.
Luke 10:19 KJV

Behold! I have given you authority and power to trample upon serpents and scorpions, and [physical and mental strength and ability] over all the power that the enemy [possesses]; and nothing shall in any way harm you.
Luke 10:19 AMPC

'Now you understand that I have imparted to you my authority to trample over his kingdom. You will trample upon every demon before you and over-come every power Satan possesses. Absolutely noth-ing will harm you as you walk in this authority.'
Luke 10:19 TPT

Some demonic attacks will continue as long as we allow them. We have been granted Heavenly authority. As a believer, you have the authority to allow on the earth what has been allowed in Heaven and forbid on the earth what has been forbidden in Heaven.

I will give you the keys of the kingdom of heaven; and whatever you bind on earth shall have been bound in heaven, and whatever you loose on earth shall have been loosed in heaven.
Matthew 16:19

Demonic activity is forbidden in Heaven. Satan and every spirit that followed him were kicked out and fell like lightning (Luke 10:18, Revelation 12:7-9).

Unlearn to Learn

People leaving the new age must unlearn what they believed, develop a proper relationship with Jesus, and learn about the Kingdom of God. Additionally, they must gain context for what they have learned and experienced concerning the spiritual realm. They may feel embarrassed or ashamed for a long time. They may feel as if they cannot talk about their experiences for fear that others may not believe them or think they are crazy. If you are reading this book and have been delivered from the occult or any other domain of darkness, know that you are not crazy or alone.

Others have experienced what you or your loved one have experienced and understand how you feel. There are things that, by God's grace, I did not experience, but I do understand. If you don't have people in your life with whom you feel you can connect with concerning this, use the contact information at the end of this book to reach out to me. I got you.

It is essential to have a community when transitioning out of the new age. By the grace of God, my wife, Valerie, understood everything I was experiencing after I left. She supported me through the various stages I went through. That's why I am intentional in cultivating community for those who have come out of the new age, occult, spiritualism, witchcraft, voodoo, or satanism, along with believers who want to experience the supernatural power of Jesus as their normal way of life. I call the community Champion University.

My Mother's Salvation

Throughout this book, I have mentioned my mother. She was deep in spiritualism and the occult, having been raised in it as I had. Despite all the events that happened in my life and hers, I know she is in Heaven with Jesus. While I did not have the honor of leading her to accept Jesus as her Savior and Lord, I am sure she did. I am sharing this as an encouragement for you to never give stop believing for the salvation of your family and friends. God is faithful and responds to your prayer.

After accepting Jesus, I went through a season where I attempted to convince my mother that what she believed was not true. It didn't work. I should have known it wouldn't because it hadn't worked on me. However, I thought I could convince her because of our relationship; the conversations only resulted in arguments. There were a few occasions, when God was restoring our relationship, when she visited Word of Life to see me. There was also an occasion when she listened to me play prophetically while visiting my apartment. I believe all of those moments were seeds planted in her soul that were watered by my faith that she would be saved.

One day, during my private time with Holy Spirit in our apartment in Cincinnati, I sensed an urgency to intercede for my mother. I went into the room where I prayed and began to pray for her in my heavenly language. I called out her name and prayed fervently. I said in English, "Do whatever it takes to free her from the occult."

While I was praying, I could sense warfare occurring in the spiritual realm. I knew the hosts of Heaven were fighting for my mother's soul. I then played prophetically on my keyboard, releasing an apostolic warlike sound. The intercession and warfare lasted for several hours. I did not stop until I felt the release from Holy Spirit and knew it was finished.

About a week later, I received a call at work; my mother had transitioned while in her home in Canada. I was heartbroken and had so many questions. I was in shock because I had just prayed for my mother's salvation. I was overcome with grief at the possibility of her soul being in hell. The grief was heavy, and I felt the weight of despair even though I was trying to be a man of strong faith.

One of the things I love about Jesus is that He comforts us during our time of need, and He does it with truth. I felt the presence of God overshadow me; He removed the intense grief and despair, replacing them with His peace. As I received His peace, I got the sense that my mother had accepted Jesus in her final moments on Earth.

Then Holy Spirit showed me something in the Scripture and confirmed what I was sensing. In Luke 23, Jesus was on the cross; two thieves were being crucified along side Him. One thief attempted to get Jesus to save Himself and come off the cross; the other said, "Jesus, remember me when You come into Your Kingdom."

And Jesus responded, "Amen, I say to you, today you will be with Me in Paradise"
Luke 23:39-43

In his final moments, the thief accepted Jesus. Even if someone accepts Jesus as Savior and Lord in their final moments, they will spend eternity with Him in Heaven.

The parable of workers in the vineyard in Matthew 20:1-16 also confirms this. That does not give us a license to live a life practicing sin; it is an assurance for us to remain in a place of faith for the salvation of those we pray for.

Holy Spirit confirmed it one additional time. While in a worship gathering at HEIRS, shortly after my mother's transition, my Apostle called me up front. He hugged me, and I began to weep. He spoke prophetically to me, saying the same thing Holy Spirit had spoken to me personally through the passage in Luke.

Those moments gave me unwavering assurance of my mother's eternal home. I had a similar experience with the LORD about my grandmother, even though no one confirmed it prophetically.

God is all-powerful and will deliver His people from the occult. We must continue to pray, believe, and obey His instructions.

CHAPTER 17

MIRACLES IN YOUR LIFE; MIRACLES IN YOUR ASSIGNMENT

God's will is that we live a supernatural life—*the right way*. The supernatural is not an occasional event that we pray and fast to experience. It is the believer's normal way of life, the standard for believers living by faith.

Too often, we equate the demonstration of God's power with a high point in a worship gathering or reduce it to something as simple as waking up and taking a breath. I am grateful for every breath God gives me; I recognize it is supposed to happen until my pre-determined time on Earth is fulfilled. I appreciate and honor God for the times when He demonstrates His power in worship gatherings. But if we wait for a high point in a worship gathering for the miraculous, we position ourselves like the man at the pool of Bethesda. We go into an environment where miracles happen and wait. While there are times when we must wait on and before the LORD, the supernatural cannot be forced and does not happen just because we waited.

The supernatural of Jesus is not an event; it is a posture and position that we live from. We do not have to wait on something God is already doing; we just align ourselves.

Empowered to Demonstrate

Before ascending to heaven, Jesus told His disciples…

> *… but you will receive power when the Holy Spirit has come upon you; and you shall be My witnesses*

*both in Jerusalem, and in all Judea and Samaria,
and even to the remotest part of the earth."*
Acts 1:8

Holy Spirit has entered the Earth, and He is available to every believer. When He comes upon the believer, He anoints us with His power. The word "power" in this passage is the Greek word *dunamis* (Strong's #1411). It means a force, specifically miraculous power. The ability of God to produce miracles through you is because of Holy Spirit. When believers pray for a miracle, they are praying for something God has already released to them.

Believers should not pray or believe for a miracle to happen *for* themselves. We should pray and believe for miracles to happen *through* us. Miracles, signs, and wonders reveal and lead people to Jesus; their sole purpose is to point people to Him.

I encourage you to use your faith to work miracles since God's miraculous power is all over you. If you need something supernatural to happen for you, understand that God will and has already done it because of the finished work of the Cross. However, this is not a miracle; it is the demonstration and enforcement of His covenant. You are in covenant relationship with God through Jesus, and the supernatural happens for you as a benefit of your relationship. It is essential to understand that what I am sharing with you is not mere semantics; it is revelation. This revelation will help you align your faith, enabling you to see greater results.

Miracles Through You, Not Just for You

When we search the gospels, we never see Jesus praying for the miraculous to happen for Himself; it always happened through Him. Jesus said that He does what He sees His Father doing (John 5:19-20). He later said that what He does we will also do and even greater works because He went back to the Father (John 14:12).

After Jesus ascended, He sent Holy Spirit, who empowers us to do what Jesus did; He performs the greater works through us.

It was the revelation of these words that caused the disciples to consistently demonstrate miracles, as we read in the Book of Acts. Everywhere the apostles and disciples went, miracles occurred.

People were healed by Peter's shadow (Acts 5:15), demons were cast out, and people were healed by Paul's handkerchief (Acts 19:11-12). Angels delivered believers from prison, people lame from birth walked, and so much more. It all happened because the power of Holy Spirit worked through them. This same power resides within us. Holy Spirit is the same today as He was then. We must believe and exercise our faith that God will use us in the miraculous.

The Miraculous as a Lifestyle

The miraculous was never meant to be contained. Just as Jesus told the first apostles that they would be His witnesses in the remotest parts of the Earth, we are to be His witnesses everywhere we go.

Witnessing is not just talking about Jesus; it is demonstrating Jesus. It is healing the sick, raising the dead, operating in our gifts, and telling them the Kingdom of God is here. We can tell a person, but we must also show them. As you operate in your gifts and are open to the miraculous happening through you, your influence will increase. People will come to you because they know God is with you. That's what happened to Jesus. People came to Him because they knew they would be healed or delivered. They also knew they would hear about the Kingdom.

Miracles Are Your Mission

You are not randomly placed where you are. You have been sent to your place of employment or called to start your business to demonstrate the Kingdom of God. This demonstration involves the miraculous. Only God can cause you to supernaturally do something that others with the same training or education level cannot do. God can cause you to produce with less effort and time than someone who does not know Him. Only God can give you the wisdom to avoid something that would cost millions of dollars or thousands of jobs.

Every area in our culture needs believers operating in the miraculous because every area needs Jesus. I believe that what we call revival, God calls normal habitation, because the intent is for it to be constant and never-ending.

Habitation is upon us, and the Kingdom of God is going to be demonstrated powerfully. It will not be contained to a worship gathering; it will happen in the marketplace and every area of cultural influence.

Ambassadors of Christ

We are living in a critical time in human history. It is the time for the believer to operate in the power of God and assume positions of influence. It is a time when we prepare the way for the LORD.

Leadership is listed as a spiritual gift in Romans 12. One of the functions of the anointing is to raise believers to positions of leadership.

You may think you are not called to lead, but you are.

You are an ambassador for Christ, a member of His Ecclesia, His governing body on Earth.

You are the head and not the tail.

You are His person of influence in the Earth.

As you operate in God's power, you will experience promotion, and people will follow you. A title may accompany that promotion, or it may not. The title does not change the reality of the assignment nor your supernatural impact.

You have been called out to advance His Kingdom! What an honor!

If you are ready to know how to lead *from* God's glory, not just *for* His glory, where you operate in the miraculous as a normal part of your life, I invite you to read the next book: *The Miracle Leader: Leading with the Power of Jesus as Your Normal.* It will be released soon.

Appendix A

Dismantling Communing with the Spirits of Biblical Figures

Let's examine 1 Samuel 28 to understand what God is communicating in this passage —and why it does not justify communing with spirits. Spiritualists often quote this passage out of context, so it is important to see it clearly through a biblical lens.

At the beginning of the chapter, the Philistines have gathered to fight Israel. The prophet Samuel had died, King Saul, seeing the Philistines, became afraid. The Scriptures record that he sought God, but the LORD did not answer him. In desperation, Saul sought a medium, even though he had, in obedience to the law, removed them from the land.

> *When Saul; inquired of the Lord, the Lord did not answer him, either by dreams or by Urim or by prophets. The Saul said to his servants, 'Seek for me a woman who is a medium, that I may go to her and inquire of her.' And his servants said, 'Behold, there is a woman who is a medium at En-dor.'*
> **1 Samuel 28:6-7**

Saul had a pattern of behavior. From early in his reign, he struggled with partial obedience and people-pleasing. He allowed the desires of the people to override God's instructions.

> *Has the Lord as much delight in burnt offerings and sacrifices as obeying the voice of the Lord? Behold, to obey is better than sacrifice, and to heed than the fat of rams. For rebellion is as the sin of divination, and insubordination is as iniquity and idolatry. Because you have rejected the word of the Lord, He has rejected you from being king.*
> **1 Samuel 15: 22-23**

Saul already had a propensity to succumb to divination. Rebellion is like the sin of divination; disobeying God is rebellion. Holy Spirit departed from Saul, and a demonic spirit began tormenting him (1 Samuel 16:14).

Disobedience, fear, oppression and desperation led Saul to consult a medium even though he knew it was wrong. He asked the woman to use a familiar spirit to bring up Samuel. When the medium saw Samuel, she cried out in fear because she was unaccustomed to seeing the spirit of a righteous person—it was unfamiliar to her. Scripture indicates Saul did not see Samuel, but heard his voice (1 Samuel 28:12-16).

Samuel's message to Saul was not new. He simply reaffirmed what God had already spoken through the prophet before his death: judgment had come; the next day Saul's sons would die.

Why had God allow this interaction? We are not told explicitly. What we do know is that this event does not condone mediumship to communicate with those who have passed away. This account shows the tragic outcome of rebellion, fear, and disobedience.

APPENDIX B

JESUS, MOSES, ELIJAH ON THE MOUNT

Some spiritualists claim that if Jesus spoke with Moses and Elijah, believers can also communicate with biblical figures who have departed. This reasoning misinterprets Scripture and ignores the context.

In Luke 16:19-31, we read the account of Lazarus and the rich man. Jesus explains that those who have departed earth cannot return to communicate with the living. In this account, Abraham told the rich man that there was a great gulf between them, making it impossible for the dead to return to give warnings, share messages, to give guidance.

What, then, about Jesus' encounter with Moses and Elijah on the Mount of Transfiguration? Yes, Jesus did speak with them, but we must pay attention to the context. Jesus was transfigured; He was in His glorified state. His divine nature had been revealed, and in the presence of three of His disciples, the Father affirmed His Son with an audible voice:

> *While he was still speaking, behold, a bright cloud*
> *overshadowed them, and suddenly a voice came*
> *out of the cloud, saying, "This is My Beloved Son,*
> *in whom I am well-pleased. Hear Him!"*
> Matthew 17:5 NKJV

The apostles witnessed this, and wanted to build three tabernacles—one for Jesus, one for Moses, one for Elijah—but God immediately redirected their focus: *Listen to Him!*

This moment revealed Jesus was the fulfillment of the Law

(Moses) and the Prophets (Elijah). It was not an invitation for believers to commune with the departed.

Some say, "If Jesus is our model and He did it, why can't I?"

Yes, Jesus is our model, but that does not mean everything He did is within our jurisdiction. We must use wisdom to know what we can do and what God has reserved within His own power.

Sadly, today, many—including well-known prophets—have claimed to have had such encounters, and even teach others how to have them. These experiences are rooted in spiritual deception. They appear supernatural but originate from familiar spirits, not Holy Spirit.

We must discern the difference between the spirit of a person and the image or likeness God may use. When *God* uses the image of a person in the Bible in a dream or a vision, He is communicating something specific.

Pray and ask Holy Spirit if the encounter was from Him, and if so, ask for the interpretation. Study the life of that person to gain more insight as to what God is speaking to you.

God calls us to pursue Him!

ABOUT THE AUTHOR

Jamal Maxsam is a husband, father, grandfather, and in passionate pursuit of God's Presence. He is the CEO of Jamal Maxsam, LLC/ Lead Like a Championprophetic leadership company that equips and ignites believers to lead with bold faith and operate in the miraculous.

Jamal serves as the Executive Pastor of HEIRS Covenant Church and business manager of The Embassy, bringing decades of experience in ministry, leadership, and spiritual activation. As a prophetic voice to a generation of miracle-minded believers, he merges faith with strategic insight to empower leaders to walk in clarity, purity, and power.

A sought-after mentor, teacher, and the host of *The Miracle Leader Podcast*, Jamal inspires believers to step boldly into their God-given assignments and partner with the Holy Spirit to see the miraculous manifest in everyday life.

When he's not leading, mentoring, or teaching, Jamal enjoys traveling to warm, palm tree-lined destinations, watching Marvel movies, and spending quality time with his family.

REFERENCES

The Oxford Dictionary: https://www.oed.com/?tl=true

Stevenson, John W. Kingdom Perspective. Retrieved from https://heirscovenant.com/kingdom-definitions/ October 16, 2024

Strong, James. *The Strong's Expanded Dictionary of Bible Words.* Nashville: Thomas Nelson Publishers, 2001.

Champion University

Champion University is a prophetic leadership mentorship program created to equip believers like you to lead with clarity, boldness, and supernatural results.

If Called Out awakened something in you—Champion University is where you'll be activated to walk it out.

Key Results of C.U.

- Clarity in Calling
- Spiritual Maturity & Purity
- Activation in the Miraculous:
- Learn to Lead from the Kingdom Perspective
- Discernment for Strategic Decisions
- Belonging in a Prophetic Leadership Community

Get Ignited

Receive mentorship today and make the miraculous your normal, not the exception

jamalmaxsam.org/cu

The
MIRACLE LEADER

Podcast with
Jamal Maxsam

A podcast dedicated to igniting faith-driven leaders to lead with boldness, strategy, and the power of God. Each week, you'll receive prophetic insights, Biblical wisdom, and practical leadership strategies to help you step fully into your divine calling.

Whether you're leading in ministry, business, or the marketplace, this show will challenge, encourage, and equip you to lead with clarity, confidence, and supernatural impact.

You weren't meant to blend in — you were born to lead with power.

Subscribe now on your favorite podcast platform — and step into the leadership God designed for you

jamalmaxsam.org/live